CURIOSITIES OF THE MIND

METIN BEKTAS

DEDICATION

This book is dedicated to my family.

CONTENTS

Introduction

I've always loved science, as far back as I can remember. I was very, very curious about how everything worked: the world, the physical universe, chemistry, law. So it was only natural to be interested in how our mind works.

– Leonard Mlodinow

Most people don't read the introduction to a book. Or maybe it's just me. But whatever the case, I've decided to keep this part short and sweet. I'll just note what needs to be noted and move on to the action. I won't tell you why you should read this book as you certainly know much better than me whether this topic is of interest to you or not. And there's no need to discuss at great length what the book is about as the title already sums it up pretty well: prepare to enter the mind's cabinet of curiosities. I've always been madly interested in the little Jedi tricks our mind is able to play and the fascinating biases we manage to carry around with us. We are highly non-linear, contradictory beings with the ability to take any simple input and turn it into a truly absurd and unpredictable output. What's not to like?

But here's the important part: this book is not a philosophical discussion on the mind. There are plenty of books out there that deal with the great questions of existence such as "Who are we?", "What is the mind?", "Do we possess a soul?", and so on. I've got nothing useful to add to this debate. Since I'm a pragmatic person who loves hard data and statistical analysis, it was my aim from the very beginning to stick as closely as possible to the experimental evidence. Instead of trying to expand on the aforementioned broad philosophical questions, I asked myself: "What do we know for sure about the mind?". Of course, there will be the inevitable speculation and generalization from time to time as there are still gaps in the experimental results. However, the choice of words and the references given will always clearly indicate whether we are talking about reliable evidence brought forth by thorough and replicable experimental studies or speculation on what the results might mean. Though we won't delve into the methods of experimental psychology, in some ways this book is as much about this subject as it is about the curious machine that is our mind. And that already concludes the introduction. Now that your seat-belt is securely fastened, let's begin the journey.

Childhood Amnesia

*I believe we accept too indifferently the fact of infantile
amnesia that is, the failure of memory for the first years of
our lives and fail to find in it a strange riddle. We forget of
what great intellectual accomplishments and of what
complicated emotions a child of four years is capable.*

– Sigmund Freud

A Fundamental Part Of Being Human

What is your earliest childhood memory? What do you feel
when recalling it? Is it a moment in time or a plotted scene?
Are you surprised that it is this particular event, and not any
other, which reverberates till today? Would your parents be
surprised to hear that this event is your earliest memory? It's
always very interesting to hear the answers to these
questions. Our earliest memory – a curious thing. Even more
curious though is the fact that no person is able to recall the
day he was born. Or the first birthday. Your earliest memory
is most likely of some event that you experienced when you
were three or four years old. Every memory before that is,
for all practical purposes, gone, deleted, kaputt. And no
matter what you do and how hard you try, these memories
will never return. It's as though you've never been an infant.
But clearly you were.

As the name suggests, childhood amnesia refers to the
inability to recall experiences before a certain critical age.
Numerous experiments have shown that this critical age, that

is, the age at the earliest memory, is usually between three and four. There are a few lucky people who manage to go back even further in time. About 1 in 8 are able to remember an event that happened to them between the ages of one and two. And 1 in 50 can even recall an event before their first birthday – quite astonishing. At the other end of the spectrum, there's a rather unlucky minority, also about 1 in 50, that cannot gain access to memories of events they experienced before the age of ten (MacDonald, Uesiliana, Hayne 2000). These are exceptions though. For the majority of us, memory begins between the ages three and four.

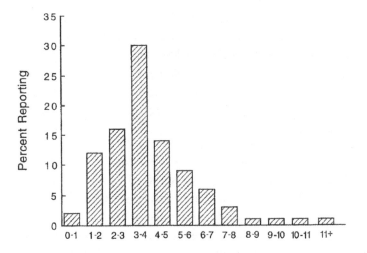

Age at earliest memory in years (MacDonald, Uesiliana, Hayne 2000)

This critical age is surprisingly stable in many ways. Most of us would assume that young adults should have fewer problems accessing the earliest memories of their lives. However, studies have revealed that 20-year-old adults are no better off than 70-year-old seniors when it comes to childhood amnesia. Both are subject to the same critical age

(Rubin, Schulkind 1997). This also holds true for gender. Although some studies have concluded that women are better at recalling pre–school memories, the difference is quite small and not always obtained in experiments. On top of that, recent findings suggest that the gender differences found in earlier studies might be a result of experimental methodology rather than a real effect. What about cultural differences? Is it possible that it is our hectic Western culture that gives rise to this curious phenomenon? Culture does have an influence on critical age, and we'll have a look at that in a moment, but again the difference is not as strong as one might suspect. The big picture that has emerged from the numerous psychological experiments is rather clear: whether you are an affluent 20-year-old Caucasian female from the US or an impoverished 70-year-old Asian male from China, you probably can't recall anything that occurred before your third birthday and most certainly can't recall your birth. Childhood amnesia is not limited to age, gender or culture, it is a fundamental part of being human.

Curious indeed. But where does it begin? Do primary–school pupils already suffer from childhood amnesia? Surprisingly, yes. Children between the ages of six and nine can commonly recall events that happened several months before the critical age found in adults, but are not able to go back further. And childhood amnesia is already fully established in children between the ages of ten and thirteen (Peterson, Grant, Boland 2005). Testing pre–school children is not possible as at this age, children have difficulty understanding the tasks given to them in experiments. So there's no way of finding out the exact age at which the infant memories get deleted. But we can say for sure that the affliction is already present when children begin their school career. Regarding early memories, their minds already work like that of a 20- or 70-year-old adult.

The Nature Of Early Memories

Besides analyzing childhood amnesia, studies have also revealed quite a bit about the nature of the earliest memories. One is inclined to assume that the earliest memory should be of an event that stands out: a birthday party, Christmas with the grandparents, the birth of a sibling or even a traumatic event such as an injury. This is certainly true for many people. However, it's just as common that the earliest memory turns out to be rather random, leaving both parents and children surprised. It's not that carefully planned and lovingly documented trip to Disneyland that ends up being the defining moment, but rather an ordinary walk to an ordinary grocery store on an ordinary day in ordinary weather.

For a minority of 1 in 5 people, the earliest memory takes them back to a traumatic event, for about the same percentage the first memory is associated with a general transition in life. Scenes of play are also quite common. Here, gender differences do surface. While girls are inclined to recall traumas, boys tend to remember scenes of play (Peterson, Grant, Boland 2005). There is still a debate on the role of emotion. Some studies have found that negative emotions were more frequent when participants recalled their earliest memory, other studies have found a balanced mix of negative and positive emotions. Also, it's not clear whether the majority of people associate emotion with their first memory. Some results indicate that emotion is a vital part of the earliest memory, while others suggest that the majority of people do not link their earliest memory to a particular emotion. This contradiction might be a result of experimental methods as in many experiments, the participants were systematically asked about emotion, skewing the result in favor of emotion.

Age group	Gender	Type of event				Total
		Trauma	Transition	Play	Other	
6–9 years	Girls	2 (10.5%)	6 (31.6%)	4 (21.0%)	7 (36.8%)	19
	Boys	5 (17.2%)	5 (17.2%)	11 (37.9%)	8 (27.6%)	29
	Both	7 (14.6%)	11 (22.9%)	15 (31.2%)	15 (31.2%)	48
10–13 years	Girls	4 (33.3%)	3 (25.0%)	1 (8.3%)	4 (33.3%)	12
	Boys	3 (15.0%)	3 (15.0%)	5 (25.0%)	9 (45.0%)	20
	Both	7 (21.9%)	6 (18.8%)	6 (18.8%)	13 (40.6%)	32
14–16 years	Girls	6 (37.5%)	1 (6.2%)	2 (12.5%)	7 (43.8%)	16
	Boys	2 (14.2%)	1 (7.1%)	5 (35.7%)	6 (42.9%)	14
	Both	8 (26.7%)	2 (6.7%)	7 (23.3%)	13 (43.3%)	30
17–19 years	Girls	6 (37.5%)	6 (37.5%)	2 (12.5%)	2 (12.5%)	16
	Boys	1 (10.0%)	2 (20.0%)	1 (10.0%)	6 (60.0%)	10
	Both	7 (26.9%)	8 (30.8%)	3 (11.5%)	8 (30.8%)	26
All ages	Girls	18 (28.6%)	16 (25.4%)	9 (14.3%)	20 (31.7%)	63
	Boys	11 (15.1%)	11 (15.1%)	22 (30.1%)	29 (39.7%)	73
	Both	29 (21.3%)	27 (19.8%)	31 (22.8%)	49 (36.0%)	136

Nature of earliest memory (Peterson, Grant, Boland 2005)

There is more clarity regarding other aspects of the first memory. For example, it is twice as likely to be a moment in time rather than a plotted scene. This might be explained by the fact that the mind of a young child has difficulty comprehending the dynamics of an event: the chronological order, cause and effect, the relationship of the people involved. So instead of the entire process, it is a snapshot of the situation that remains. Another noteworthy aspect is that the early memories seem surprisingly accurate. To test the accuracy, some childhood amnesia studies included the feedback of parents. In most cases the parents were able to confirm the details of the earliest memory given by their children (though the estimated age at this event often differed by a few months). Sometimes the earliest memory did turn out to be a false memory though – another curiosity of the mind.

It happens quite often that our memory fails us. We want to recall one particular name, one particular recipe, one particular date – but alas, we just cannot gain access to the relevant part of our mind. Often trying harder to remember will do the trick. However, sometimes there's nothing to do but to let the mind do its thing and wait for the memory to return. This is normal forgetting, a phenomenon we are all aware of and familiar with. What we are less familiar with, though also quite common, is that our mind can and does create false memories: memories of events we think we experienced, but never did. This can be something banal such as believing we put the keys on the table (never happened) or something more substantial such as thinking we came up with a certain idea (someone else did) or believing we saw that man at the scene of the crime (he wasn't there). Loftus 1995 showed that not only does that happen more often than we suspect, it's also quite simple to induce false memories by giving the right cues. Hence, it's a good idea to include parents in childhood amnesia experiments.

Parents, Culture And Gender

Including parents turned out to be enlightening in many other ways as well. The nature and degree of childhood amnesia depends strongly on the narrative style of the parents. Research has shown that there are two distinct styles, high–elaborative and low–elaborative, and that most parents stick to one of the two styles throughout their child's development. High–elaborative parents provide their children with vivid descriptions of past events, encouraging them to remember every detail, whereas low–elaborative parents focus more on the big picture and tend to repeat questions over and over when prompting their children to remember certain events. Not surprisingly, the high–

elaborative style has proven to exhibit a positive effect on the ability to recall events from early childhood (Peterson, McCabe 1994).

The influence of narrative style is also a factor in spawning cultural differences in childhood amnesia. Tape recordings of Caucasian and Korean mothers showed that not only are Caucasian mothers more likely to exhibit a high–elaborative style, they also talk to their children three times more often about past events than Korean mothers (Mullen, Yi 1995). It should not come as a surprise then that for Asian adults, especially female Asian adults, the critical age is closer to six years rather than the commonly found three to four years. But it's not just the critical age. Another experiment (Han 1998) has found that the recollections of Korean children were relatively sparse compared to the accounts given by Caucasian children of the same age. The Korean children seemed to copy the low–elaborative style of their parents, focusing on the main events and giving very few details surrounding those.

So the supposedly hectic Western culture with its "don't look back"–attitude does a surprisingly good job at encouraging children to maintain early childhood memories, but it is by no means in the leading position. For example, a study with Maori adults revealed an average critical age of around two and a half years, a whole year less than what is usually found in experiments (MacDonald, Uesiliana, Hayne 2000). On top of that, their accounts of past events proved to be very vivid and outstandingly rich in detail. This was especially true for female Maoris. So there is room for improvement, both for the Western and Asian culture.

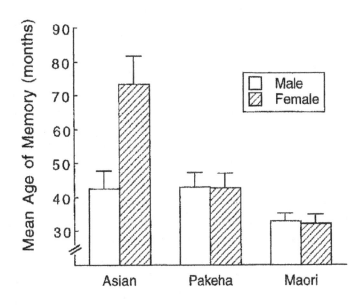

Critical age in months across cultures (MacDonald, Uesiliana, Hayne 2000)

Now let's turn our attention to gender. As noted, the picture that emerged from the numerous experiments on childhood amnesia is quite hazy regarding gender differences. There are studies which claim that girls and women are better at recalling early events than boys and men, studies which did not find such a difference in gender and other studies, mainly those performed in Asian countries, in which men clearly had the upper hand. So what's going on? Why the confusing results?

Some psychologists have suggested that the experimental method plays a crucial role in bringing forth or masking gender differences. This is certainly plausible considering the following results. When participants were asked to put their earliest memory into writing, women performed better in the sense that their average age at the earliest memory proved to be lower than that of the male participants. However, when the participants reported their earliest memory orally, this difference simply vanished, showing that gender differences are indeed tied to methodology (Peterson, Warren, Nguyen, Noel 2010). While this might not be able to explain the significant gender differences obtained in Asian countries, it does shed light on the other conflicting results.

Of course the outcome of the experiment mentioned above is interesting beyond aspects of gender as it demonstrates that the age at the earliest memory reported by participants depends on how it is reported, a phenomenon most of us would not expect. For both men and women the critical age was significantly lower when the memories were reported orally. To be specific, it was half a year lower for women and even a full year lower for men. Why the difference? One explanation: recalling early memories takes a lot of time and effort and people might be more willing to dig deep in a more personal setting such as a face–to–face conversation. But further experiments are necessary to unearth gender differences and the effects of methodology on critical age.

Groups	Women		Men	
	M	*SD*	*M*	*SD*
Written/group task	38.6	9.9	43.3	10.8
Oral/individual task	31.1	11.1	31.4	11.6

Age at earliest memory in months and method of reporting (Peterson, Warren, Nguyen, Noel 2010). M = Mean, SD = Standard Deviation.

The Self And Autobiographical Memories

Up to this point we have avoided the most important question: why are we not able to recall our birth or our first birthday? What is it that leads to the formation of this impenetrable wall between you and your early self? A commonly heard first guess is that one can't recall what isn't there. We are not able to recall our first birthday because our memory was not functional at this early age. Nothing got stored and thus there's nothing to recall. The theory seems plausible at first sight, but is it true? Research has provided an answer: no, this explanation is too simplistic. Infants and pre–school children are most certainly able to form memories, both short– and long–term (Hartshorn et al. 1998). So the plausible first guess has to be abandoned – sort of. Sort of, because there's still some truth in our logic.

In the above paragraph we have assumed all memories to be born alike, a very crude assumption. Most modern theories on childhood amnesia take a closer look at the many different forms of memory that psychologists were able to identify experimentally. For example, Howe and Courage (1997) put the emphasis on the so–called autobiographical memory. This is the part of our memory that is responsible for storing everything we have personally experienced ("I touched the stove, it was hot"), while mere facts ("Stoves can be hot") are collected and stored separately. It seems obvious that such autobiographical memories can only be formed if the concept of the self is present. No self, no personal experience – fair enough. And since the concept of the self does not begin developing before the age of three, quite close to the age at the earliest memory found by experiments, this would explain why we can't recall any personal experiences from early childhood. We touched the stove and felt the heat, but without any understanding of "I" and "you", all we remember is that stoves can be hot. Certainly an important lesson that will spare us painful experiences later on, but not an autobiographical memory.

Note that this theory agrees quite well with the result that people who grew up in a Western setting can commonly get closer to their younger self than people raised in Asian countries. The Western culture is characterized by a strong focus on individuality, promoting the early development of an autonomous sense of the self, while the Asian culture prefers to put the spotlight on the idea of the collective. It should not come as a surprise then that the sense of self, and with it the possibility of collecting personal experiences, emerges at an earlier age when a child absorbs the Western mentality.

All of this is very plausible, but one should mention that at this point, there is no universally accepted explanation of childhood amnesia and it will most likely remain this way until the relevant questions are settled. How does memory work? What neurological changes occur in our early development and how are they related to the inability to remember our early self? What role does language play? There is still so much to learn and that is a fantastic thing.

Sources And Further Reading:

Infantile / Childhood Amnesia (M. L. Howe)

Cross–cultural and Gender Differences in Childhood Amnesia (Shelley MacDonald, Kimberly Uesiliana, Harlene Hayne)

Parent–child relationship quality and infantile amnesia in adults (Carole Peterson, Duyen T. Nguyen)

Infantile Amnesia and Gender: Does the Way we Measure it Matter? (Carole Peterson, Kelly Warren, Duyen T. Nguyen, Melanie Noel)

What Infant Memory Tells us about Infantile Amnesia (Andrew N. Meltzoff)

Memory for the Events of Early Childhood (Madeline J. Eacott)

IKEA Effect

"The highest reward for man's toil is not what he gets for it, but what he becomes by it."

– John Ruskin

Labor Leads To Love

Suppose you want to buy a new PC. Checking your bank account, you find that your budget is rather limited at the moment, so you search the internet for a used one. You happen to come across my offer. A good processor, large hard drive, nice video card, all of this for $ 300. You contact me and try to get an even better deal. Since I'm in a pretty good mood, I'm willing to make the deal sweeter. If you agree to come pick the computer up, sparing me the trouble of bringing it to the post office, I'll give it to you for ... $ 350. Sounds good? Probably not. So I expect you to put in extra effort AND pay more? No deal.

Just recently I browsed eBay for a model of the Boeing 747, the famous Jumbo Jet. While you can find a nice–looking, assembled model for $ 10, model kits that require assembly start at around $ 20. So they expect me to put in extra effort AND pay more? Indeed they do. For many people assembling model aircrafts is a hobby. They enjoy the peace of mind the labor brings. They could just buy an assembled model at a lower price, but they prefer to put it together themselves, even if it costs a bit more. From a purely economic point of view, this seems odd. But from a human perspective, it makes sense.

Here's another example of this very human phenomenon: Pick Your Own farms. If you love strawberries, you can always go to the nearest grocery store and buy them at a low price. Alternatively, if you are willing to put in more effort and pay extra money, you can travel to a Pick Your Own farm and personally pick these tasty fruits in the hot summer sun. To a completely rational person with a computer–like mind this is a no–brainer. Why put in extra effort AND pay more? Yet, in some ways the alternative is attractive as well. Walking out onto the open field that stretches to the horizon, bounded only by an infinite blue sky, feeling the dry, warm earth under your feet as you pick the strawberries – that's certainly worth something. You can bet that these strawberries will taste better than the ones you buy at the grocery store and not just because they are fresh.

In both examples, the increase in value we assigned to a certain end–product (the model aircraft, the strawberries) came as a result of labor that brought us joy. Surprisingly, joy is not even the key element here. Suppose you get two identical tables for your room, one assembled by you, the other assembled by a helpful neighbor. One year later you need space for a piano in your room, meaning that you have to get rid of one of the tables. Which one will you keep? Most likely the one you have personally assembled. And not because you enjoyed assembling it so much, but because you put effort into this task. The effort alone created a hard–to–define "bond" between you and the table. Welcome to the IKEA effect, where labor leads to love.

From a rational perspective, this effect shouldn't exist. We are offered a certain product at a certain price. If the offer is changed, requiring us to put in extra work, we expect a reduction in price to reflect this. The final price should be initial price minus the cost of our additional labor. Think back to the computer. I offered it to you for $ 300. Now if you agree to pick it up, requiring a two–hour drive that prevents you from spending quality time with your family, you expect me to lower the price to take the extra effort into account. The rational you certainly wouldn't expect or accept the $ 350 counter–offer. However, the irrational you, the you that is not purely driven by maximizing profit, might like the idea of having to work hard for luxuries and taking the opportunity to enjoy the freedom of the open road, where, as you know, anything is possible. All of this might cause you to overvalue the computer, just as the hobbyist overvalued the model aircraft and the nature–loving person overvalued the strawberries. Note that when we say "overvalue", we mean that the good is assigned a value above its market value, no moral judgment is implied.

Cognitive Dissonances

Why do we value a product more when we put effort into it? One approach of explaining this phenomenon is via the concept of cognitive dissonance. The term cognitive dissonance refers to the discomfort a person experiences when subject to two contradicting beliefs or ideas at the same time. According to Festinger, a person experiencing such discomfort will avoid situations which might amplify the cognitive dissonance and adjust his or her beliefs in an attempt to eliminate this state of tension.

An impressive example of this is provided by people who have the misfortune of belonging to a doomsday cult. Through the brainwashing of a charismatic leader, they come to believe that on the date X the world will end. This is accepted by loyal cult members as an undeniable truth. Of course, at some point in the future, date X will arrive and pass and the world will, undeniably, still exist. Now two very powerful contradicting thoughts, "the world will end on date X" and "X has passed but nothing happened", are competing in the person's mind. The person will then attempt to eliminate the discomfort caused by this contradiction. Ideally, he or she will come to understand that the charismatic leader is nothing but a flashy con–man and rejoin society. However, overly committed cultists will argue that the world did not end because of their actions (Festinger 1957). The aliens saw the devoted few and decided to spare Earth. This also successfully resolves the cognitive dissonance, though not in a particularly healthy manner (resolving dissonances of the mind is a common source of comforting lies and delusions).

Example of cognitive dissonance – how do you think he'll resolve it?

Cognitive dissonance, successfully but sub–optimally resolved

What does this have to do with the IKEA effect? We're getting there. Suppose you are keen on joining a seemingly interesting local discussion group. However, the group has not made joining easy. You have to go through several hazing rituals: solve a differential equation, run naked through the streets screaming "Eureka", deliver a baby in a stranded car, wrestle a Grizzly bear in the Rocky Mountains, cross the Sahara desert, etc ... Since you really, really want to join this supposedly fabulous group, you put in the effort and perform all the tasks. Then some spectacular day they confirm that you are now a proud member of this discussion group. So far, so good ... the only problem: all they do is talk about the weather and it's extremely boring. This discussion is not what you expected. All this effort, for what? You are now subject to cognitive dissonance. The enormous effort put into completing the tasks made you expect a great reward (we will have fascinating discussions), but the reality looks different (we are only talking about the weather). Resolve this.

High Expectations versus Low Rewards

This type of cognitive dissonance, expecting high reward as a result of great effort and in reality getting low reward despite the great effort, is commonly resolved using effort justification. We make ourselves believe that the low reward wasn't that bad after all. Sure, we didn't expect to talk about the weather non–stop, but meteorology is an exciting field and there's a lot to be learned. Many experiments have confirmed this Jedi mind–trick. For example, Gerard and Mathewson (1966) found that participants who were subjected to relatively strong electrical shocks to be able to join a dull discussion group had a more positive attitude towards this group than those who only had to endure mild shocks or no shocks at all. The effort (in this case, pain) created expectations that were not met and the dissonance between expecting high reward and getting low reward was resolved by believing that the low reward was actually not that bad. The other two participant groups did not have to deal with this dissonance as their hazing ritual took less effort and thus the need to believe that the low reward was ything but a low reward was not created.

Now we can apply this to the IKEA effect. Suppose you buy a table and put in the effort to assemble it at home. This builds up expectations that would not be there had you simply bought the table in a fully assembled state. However, there is no high reward, at least no reward higher than that of an already assembled table. So the higher reward expected from putting in the extra effort is met by the reality of a relatively low reward. Well, it's a table, what did you expect? Automatically and sub–consciously applying the effort justification mind–trick, you assign the table a higher value to get rid of this dissonance. Peace of mind is achieved and the IKEA effect born.

Now we can also see why joy is not a key ingredient. It's the mere effort that leads to the high expectations and the resulting cognitive dissonance, neither joy nor the possibility of product customization are a requirement. However, joy actually provides another elegant way out of the dissonance dilemma. Instead of overvaluing the end–product to resolve our high versus low reward problem, we can "undervalue" the effort and then gladly accept the low reward. How do we undervalue effort? By seeing the joy in it. If you really enjoyed assembling the table, so what if the end–product is just ... well, a common table? If you really enjoyed running naked through the streets and wrestling the Grizzly bear, so what if the discussion group is more boring than expected? Unfortunately, it seems that this uplifting way out of the high versus low reward dissonance is less common than the IKEA effect, that is, overvaluing the outcome. It shouldn't be.

Self-Perception Theory

Cognitive dissonance is not the only psychological factor relevant for the occurrence of the IKEA effect though. Another interesting aspect of it is self–perception. Usually we believe that people act a certain way because of who they are. A person helps an old lady cross the busy street because he or she is compassionate. The teacher gives the students plenty of time to finish an exercise because he or she is patient. We recycle because we care about the environment. So first comes the personality trait or attitude and then the behavior. However, experiments have revealed that there is more to the story.

You might have heard the following tip that turns this common wisdom on its head. If you feel depressed, just start smiling. The good feelings will follow even if you don't see a rational reason to feel good at the moment. This actually works and demonstrates a curious thing: we constantly observe our own behavior and draw conclusions from the observations (Laird, Bresler 1992). Usually this is a subconscious process, but at some point you might have consciously noticed that. Have you ever been surprised about how you acted in a certain situation? Some little thing might have made you more angry than it should have and you thought to yourself: "man, I'm really impatient". You perceived your own behavior and deduced from that who and what you are.

Numerous studies have shown that this kind of self–perception is surprisingly common. So all of the examples mentioned above work the other way as well, but in a less obvious fashion. The person "observes" himself helping the old lady cross the street and subconsciously infers that he is quite compassionate. The teacher notices that she gives the students plenty of time to finish the exercises and concludes that she must be a patient person. You observe yourself recycling and deduce that you care about the environment (conveniently not acknowledging that you probably wouldn't do it had the city not made recycling so easy – we often fail to recognize the circumstances and social pressures). We do what we are, but we also are what we do. And if we pretend to be someone else, over time we might just become someone else.

From the perspective of self–perception theory, we can see that the IKEA effect provides an excellent opportunity to find out who we are and to feel good about ourselves. While assembling the model aircraft, the hobbyist observes his labor and is able to deduce and confirm that he is a careful and patient person, which is probably true considering this choice of hobby. He would not have been able to feel this reassurance had he simply bought the already assembled model at a lower price. We can apply similar reasoning to the person visiting the Pick Your Own farm. Feeling the warm earth under your feet and drops of sweat rolling down your face is a powerful way to confirm that you value nature and hard work. You buy the strawberries as much as you buy the reassurance and that is certainly not something you can get at the nearest grocery store.

Of Origami Frogs and Men

Note that the IKEA effect does not just apply to products made by others, but also to our own creations. And this is where it gets really difficult. Suppose you write and produce a song. How good is it compared to songs written and produced by professional composers, those who have been in this business for decades? At some point in your life you might paint a picture and ask yourself: how good is it compared to paintings by professional artists? And I find myself asking: how enjoyable is my book compared to that of a bestselling New York Times writer? Clearly we put effort into our own creations and this brings the danger of the IKEA effect: overvaluing the result of our own labor.

The experiment by Norton, Mochon, Ariely (2011) is an impressive demonstration of this. In it, they asked 106 participants to create an origami frog or crane and offered them to buy their own creations. They also asked other participants to bid on these creations. It turned out that participants were willing to pay around $ 0.23 for their own creations, but only $ 0.05 for creations made by other participants – a very large difference. Being aware of the IKEA effect, this is in line with what we expected: personal effort is put in, value increases. But there's more to the story. The experimentators brought in a few experts who were also asked to craft origami frogs and cranes. On average, participants offered to pay $ 0.27 for the expert creations. So the participants assigned their own amateurish creations roughly the same market value as the expert creations, but did recognize that the amateurish creations made by other participants had a lower market value than those created by the experts.

Of course, companies have already shown great interest in these results and are keen on applying the IKEA effect. Let the customer do part of the labor AND get more money? You certainly won't hear the managers saying no. More and more, the customer is seen not just as a mere recipient of goods, but rather as the co–creator of a product. However, it's not as simple as putting "you'll have to assemble this yourself" on the box and watch the money roll in. The IKEA effect is a retrospective phenomenon. You overvalue the table <u>after</u> you put in the labor, not before. If someone asked you before buying the table whether you want to personally assemble it or not, you'd probably prefer the already assembled table. Only for labor that brings joy would such a direct approach work. Thus, when trying to guide customers to the IKEA effect, an indirect route has to be chosen. One example: elevate their energy levels using caffeine, this will make them more willing to put in more effort (Gibbs, Drolet 2003). However, one has to wonder about the morality of such a devious attitude towards the customer. I'm sure that no customer likes being the recipient of cheap parlor tricks.

Sources And Further Reading:

The IKEA effect: When Labor Leads to Love (Michael I. Norton, Daniel Mochon, Dan Ariely)

The Theory of Cognitive Dissonance (Adam Kowol)

Cognitive Consequences of Forced Compliance (Leon Festinger, James M. Carlsmith)

What Does Being Initiated Severely into a Group do? The Role of Rewards (Caroline Kamau)

False Consensus Effect

The object of life is not to be on the side of the majority, but to escape finding oneself in the ranks of the insane.

– Marcus Aurelius

Bungee Jumping Enthusiasts Are Biased

You don't smoke, you enjoy being with the family and you drink a glass of wine every now and then. Do you think these habits say a lot about who you are? How common do you think these habits are? What percentage of the population does not smoke? Enjoys being with the family? Drinks a glass of wine from time to time? Unfortunately, I have to admit that I do smoke and one might suspect that this can cause my estimate for the size of the non-smoking population to be different from yours. You might say 80 % of the population does not smoke, while my guess would rather be somewhere around 70 %. It's important to remember though that both of us are biased when trying to come up with the estimate, you by not smoking, I by smoking.

Numerous experiments have confirmed that people consider their habits, beliefs and behavioral patterns to be more common, and thus less telling of their own character, than people who do not share this habit, belief or behavioral pattern. This is referred to as the false consensus effect. A non-smoker will consider the non-smoking population to be larger than the smoker. A family person tends to believe a higher percentage enjoys being with the family than a person who does not like to spend time with the family. And people who enjoy alcohol give a higher estimate for the percentage of people who also like to drink than those who dislike alcohol.

I encourage you to reread the definition and examples to understand what the false consensus effect does <u>not</u> mean, as it is quite easy to misunderstand. It does not mean that people are inclined to think that their habits, beliefs and behavioral patterns are shared by a majority. For example, a bungee jumping enthusiast is probably fully aware that only a minority of the population has the same keen interest in extreme thrills. What the false consensus effect does is equipping his estimate for the commonness of the love for extreme sports with a bias. In a similar fashion, people who cheat on their partners probably realize that this behavioral pattern is not shared by the majority, but their estimate for the percentage of the population that does engage in such questionable behavior is biased (Holmes 1968).

Another important aspect to keep in mind is that the definition of the false consensus effect does not go into who is overestimating and who is underestimating the true percentage. As stated, a non-smoker will consider the non-smoking population to be larger than the smoker. While the non-smoker claims that 80 % do not smoke, the smoker says this number should be closer to 70 %. The true percentage might be somewhere in between, in which case the non-smoker overestimated the size of the non-smoking population and the smoker underestimated it. But it's also possible that both overestimate or underestimate this number. The true percentage of non-smokers might be 60 %, in which case both overestimate the number, or 90 %, in which case both underestimate it. The false consensus effect does <u>not</u> claim that the non-smoker will overestimate the number of non-smokers, it only states that the non-smoker gives a higher number than the smoker. It's a relative effect, not an absolute one.

What Would You Do?

Let's have a look at a classic experimental study on the false consensus effect to see it in action. In 1976, Lee Ross, David Greene and Pamela House presented the following story and questions to 80 Stanford undergraduates:

As you are leaving your neighborhood supermarket, a man in a business suit asks whether you like shopping in that store. You reply quite honestly that you do like shopping there and indicate that in addition to being close to your home, the supermarket seems to have very good meats and produces at reasonably low prices. The man then reveals that a videotape crew has filmed your comments and asks you to sign a release allowing them to use the unedited film for a TV commercial that the supermarket chain is preparing.

- Would you sign the release?

- What percentage of your peers do you estimate would sign the release?

What answers would you provide? Take a moment to think about it before reading on. It turned out that of the 80 undergraduates, 66 % would sign the release and 34 % would not. On average, those who indicated that they would be willing to sign the release estimated that 76 % of their peers would do the same, so they overestimated the true percentage (66 %) by 10 %. The students who said that they would refuse to sign the release in this situation estimated that 57 % of their peers would give their signature, underestimating the true percentage (66 %) by 9 %. Note that despite underestimating the true percentage, the "refusers" did realize that their choice is not shared by the majority. Let's have a look at the second story in the experiment, also presented to 80 undergraduates:

You arrive for the first day of class in a course in your major area of study. The professor says that the grade in your course will depend on a paper due the final day of the course. He gives the class the option of two alternatives upon which they must vote. They can either do papers individually in the normal way or they can work in teams of three persons who will submit a single paper between them. You are informed that he will still give out the same number of A's, B's, C's, etc ... but that in the first case every student will be graded individually, while in the second case all three students who work together get the same grade.

- What would you vote for, individual or group papers?

- What percentage of your peers do you estimate would vote for individual papers?

Again, take a minute to find your own answers to these questions, then read on. The analysis revealed that of the 80 undergraduates, 80 % would choose the individual paper while the remaining 20 % would prefer the group paper. The students who chose the individual paper estimated that 67 % of their peers would do the same, underestimating the true percentage (80 %) by 13 %. Students who preferred the group paper were off by even more. They estimated that only

46 % would choose the individual paper, underestimating the true percentage (80 %) by 35 % and falsely believing themselves to be part of the majority. They would have been in for a surprise, had there been an actual vote on this matter.

Story	Rater's own choice in hypothetically described situation	n (%)	Estimates of consensus: estimated percentage of raters who would choose		F
			Option 1	Option 2	
Supermarket story	Sign release	53 (66%)	75.6	24.4	17.7
	Not sign release	27 (34%)	57.3	42.7	
Term paper story	Choose individual paper	64 (80%)	67.4	32.6	16.5
	Choose group paper	16 (20%)	45.9	54.1	
Traffic ticket story	Pay speeding fine	37 (46%)	71.8	28.2	12.8
	Contest charge	43 (54%)	51.7	48.3	
Space program story	Vote for cutback	32 (40%)	47.9	52.1	4.9
	Vote against cutback	48 (60%)	39.0	61.0	
Summary of four stories[a]	Choose option 1	186 (58%)	65.7	34.3	49.1
	Choose option 2	134 (42%)	48.5	51.5	

[a] Unweighted average of means for four stories.

Ross, Greene, House (1976)

The data demonstrates what we mentioned in the first paragraphs. Though the false consensus effect can lead a person with a minority opinion to believe the he or she is part of the majority, this is not the essence of the effect. And while the question of who overestimates and who underestimates the true percentage is quite interesting, it is not the main point. The core of the effect is that people with opinion X give a higher estimate for the percentage of people having this opinion X than people who do not have this opinion X.

Note though that the implications of this effect go far beyond the lifeless numerical estimate. If you believe certain habits, beliefs and behavioral patterns to be more common, you believe them to be less deviant and less telling of character. On the other hand, giving a smaller estimate for the true percentage implies believing that this certain habit, belief and behavioral pattern is relatively unusual (moral judgment included) and rich with implications about a person's character. Studies show that these kinds of implications, the stretch from pure number to psychological quality, are very commonplace. Thus, the false consensus effect is certainly more than just the inability to provide a good estimate to a mathematical quantity. It's true that objectively commonness is just a number, but in our minds it is also a moral judgment. Common is safe, trustworthy and reassuring, uncommon is (can be) dangerous, suspicious and unsettling.

A Powerful Defense Mechanism

Let's move on to the question of why. What psychological mechanisms lead to the formation of the false consensus effect? We should note that the false consensus effect is basically projection in action (say it out loud, a neat rhyme). The effect demonstrates that those who have a certain belief X are more likely to project this belief X onto others than those who do not have it. Hence, to understand why the effect arises, we have to find out why we feel the need to ascribe our own characteristics onto others in the first place.

Classical psychology mainly focused on projection as a defense mechanism by means of denial. A person denies an aspect of his own attitude or behavior and transfers it onto others, successfully relieving himself of the associated guilt or shame in the process. For example, in an argument with your partner you might have found yourself accusing him or her of making a mountain out of a molehill, while careful reflection later on revealed that you were the one doing just that. Another example: fundamentalist christians commonly accuse people supporting the scientific theory of evolution of being religious zealots, a pretty transparent case of projection. The psychologist Carl Gustav Jung noted that such projections often lead to counter-projections, a dynamic which can quickly turn a conflict into a "projection fest", with accusations flying back and forth that inadvertently reveal more about the accuser than the accused.

However, the false consensus effect proves that the classical perspective on projection is too narrow. The non-smoker is most certainly aware of his habit and does not deny this habit when projecting it onto others. Despite that, one can safely assume that reaching a more desirable emotional state is also a relevant factor in this form of projection. For example, an honest person obviously feels more comfortable in a world of honest people than among dishonest peers. And for the dishonest person, projecting this trait onto others helps to dilute the moral failure, the classic "but everybody's doing it" defense. So even without the element of denial, projection can serve as a powerful defense mechanism.

The elimination of denial as part of the projection also opens up the possibility of using projection as a tool for enhancing self-esteem. Research shows (Bauman, Geher 2002) that we feel the constant need to compare ourselves with our peers in order to find validation and build up self-esteem. While looking inward can also serve as a source for self-esteem, it seems that the vast majority of us cannot do without this external reference. We maintain and further self-esteem first and foremost by identifying traits in ourselves that we believe to be highly valued by the people around us. Hence, the honest person's self-esteem can greatly profit from believing honesty to be a relatively common, and thus highly appreciated, personality trait. At the same time, the failure to recognize the true commonness can limit the damage to the dishonest person's self-esteem by creating the illusion that honesty, while certainly an appreciated and positive quality, is less common and thus not so highly valued.

Friends - A Biased Sample Of Mankind

We should also mention the role of numerical feedback in upholding the false consensus effect. Clearly, it would just take you a few minutes to look up the percentage of non-smokers, settling this question in a satisfactory manner and eliminating your bias. But there are several problems with this seemingly obvious solution to the false consensus problem. For one, finding or even defining the corresponding number is not always that simple. How common is depression? What is the percentage of people suffering from depression in the US? Browsing the internet, you will find that estimates range from anywhere between 1 % to 10 %, leaving lots of room for a biased perspective, even for the well-informed. Secondly, we often don't feel strongly enough about a certain topic or have the time to actually research the number. Thus, reliable numerical feedback, which could serve as an efficient remedy for and welcome reminder of the false consensus bias, seems to be the exception rather than the rule.

The lack of numerical feedback wouldn't be so bad if it weren't for what psychologists refer to as selective exposure. How do you choose your friends? Do you simply point at a random person and say "you are my friend now"? Clearly it doesn't work like that. When it comes to choosing friends, all of us have certain strategies. Some prefer being around outgoing people, others prefer to surround themselves with thinkers (though the one does not necessarily exclude the other). But whatever your strategy, it's certainly not a fully random approach. Hence, the people that define our social world make up a biased sample of mankind, a sample that we often use to form ideas about people in general. It's easy to see that this selective exposure and the tendency to generalize can lead us to draw incorrect conclusions. For example, if you feel that nowadays people are more open-minded than they were ten years ago, it might be because society as a whole has indeed become more liberal and progressive. But beware, it's just as likely that it is your biased sample that has gotten even more biased over the years. So again we're back to the need of reliable numerical feedback, which is usually pretty difficult to come by even with Google as our faithful servant. Finding a trustworthy time-series of the percentage of open-minded people? Good luck with that.

Before concluding the chapter on the false consensus effect, we take the opportunity to mention another psychological phenomenon that is commonly regarded as its counterpart: pluralistic ignorance. In this case a person overestimates the group's endorsement of a certain habit, belief or behavioral pattern and decides to go along with it despite rejecting it in private. This can lead to the awkward situation that a belief gains the public majority when in reality there's only a minority honestly supporting it. A classic example of this is racial segregation. During the civil rights movement, American whites overestimated the support for segregation among their peers and accordingly, many decided to publicly speak out against integration despite privately favoring it (O'Gorman, 1979). A more recent example of pluralistic ignorance is the political correctness trend. People are inclined to give in to ideas deemed politically correct by the majority to avoid being misperceived by their peers as cold-hearted, bigoted or racist, even if the doubts they harbor in private are reasonable and not motivated by a racial considerations (Boven, 2000).

Sources And Further Reading:

The "False Consensus Effect": An Egocentric Bias in Social Perception and Attribution Processes (Lee Ross, David Greene, Pamela House)

Attitude Importance and the False Consensus Effect (Leandre R. Fabrigar, Jon A. Krosnick)

The False Consensus Effect: A Meta-Analysis of 115 Hypothesis Tests (Brian Mullen, Jennifer L Atkins, Debbie S Champion, Cecelia Edwards, Dana Hardy, John E Story, Mary Vanderklok)

Freudian Defense Mechanisms and Empirical Findings in Modern Social Psychology: Reaction Formation, Projection, Displacement, Undoing, Isolation, Sublimation, and Denial (Roy F. Baumeister, Karen Dale, and Kristin L. Sommer)

Actor - Observer Bias

I would love to be able to read minds. How cool would it be to get inside peoples' heads and figure out what they're thinking? I guess that's a good and a bad thing.

– Kelli Berglund

Everybody's To Blame Except You

Suppose you have dinner with a close friend at a lovely Italian restaurant. You enjoy the food and the philosophical conversation with your buddy. But at the table next to you, trouble arises. Another guest is obviously not pleased with the bill the waiter presented to him. He demands to see the manager and once the boss arrives, things get really hot. The angry guest complains about the long wait, crappy food (his words), unfriendly waiter, etc ... So much for your quiet evening. What do you think about this guest? My guess: you think that he is an angry, belligerent and impatient person who doesn't care about how his temper affects the people around him. Certainly not someone you'd like to have in your family or at your workplace.

Scene change. You are on your way to a computer store to pick up the printer you ordered last week. Your old printer has failed you at the worst possible moment (don't they always?) and you need the new one urgently to print out your report. If that weren't bad enough, your tooth has been aching the whole week, but the thought of going to the dentist is even worse than the intense pain. When you enter the computer store, the clerk informs you that the printer hasn't arrived yet and asks you to come back after the weekend. After the weekend?! The printer should have arrived two days ago! You demand to see the owner and once he arrives, you give him a piece of your mind: long wait, crappy products (your words), unfriendly clerks, ... What do you think the guy waiting in line behind you thinks about you? My guess: he thinks that you are an angry, belligerent and impatient person who doesn't care about how his temper affects the people around him. Certainly not someone you'd like to have in your family or at your workplace. Are you this person?

I'm pretty sure your assessment of the situation is a bit different. You are normally a calm, harmonic and patient person who is very considerate of other people. Just yesterday you helped an old lady cross the street even though you were already late. Would an impatient and inconsiderate person do this? Of course not. The outburst was a result of situational factors. The unreasonable deadline for the report set by your boss, the failure of the printer, the pain, the incompetence of the computer store. Who wouldn't get angry?

So, there it is, the actor-observer bias, in all its glory. If we do something, act in a certain way, we tend to explain the behavior using situational forces: an unreasonable boss, being in a hurry, pain, money problems, bad weather or even the full moon. We clearly see all the elements that led up to this particular moment and (try to) identify the relevant elements that explain why we did what we did. However, if we observe someone else doing something, we are inclined to use personality traits to understand the behavior: angry, belligerent, patient, impatient, friendly, unfriendly, etc ...

Fidel Castro's Army Of Students

Examples of the actor-observer bias are plenty. Saulnier, Perlman (1981) interviewed 60 inmates, who at the time were incarcerated in a medium-security penitentiary in Canada, and asked them why they committed the crimes. While the inmates were keen on emphasizing the external and situational aspects leading up to the crime (money problems, family issues, opportunity), their counselors saw the criminal behavior of the inmates more as a result of personality (aggressiveness, selfishness, impulsivity). A similar situation was found when interviewing psychologists and their clients. The majority of clients explained their behavior in terms of situational factors, while their psychologists preferred to see the same behavior as a consequence of personality. In case you are not convinced yet, here's another straight-forward example: Nisbett, Caputo (1971) requested college students to write a short text detailing why they had chosen their field of study. Afterward, they were asked to write a similar text explaining what made their best friends choose their majors. It turned out that the participants viewed the choices their friends made more in terms of disposition than their own, confirming the actor-observer bias.

The actor-observer bias in action

Surprisingly, it seems that we have a tendency for biased observations even when the actor's behavior takes place under extreme external constraints that leave the actor practically no choice to behave differently. Jones, Harris (1967) presented participants with anti- and pro-Castro essays presumably written by college students as part of an assignment. It was made clear to the participants that, while in some cases the students were free to choose a side, in other cases the students were given no choice and instructed to write a defense of Castro's Cuba. The hypothetical students had access to study materials to research the topic before and while writing the essays, ruling out knowledge as an assessment factor. Despite this and despite the fact that a related questionnaire showed that the external constraints were recognized by the participants, their opinion of the students was noticeably affected by the essay, even in the no choice condition. They inferred pro-Castro attitudes where logically no such inferences should be made. As Jones and Nisbett noted, it seems that we pretty much take the behavior of others at face value, ignorant of situational forces.

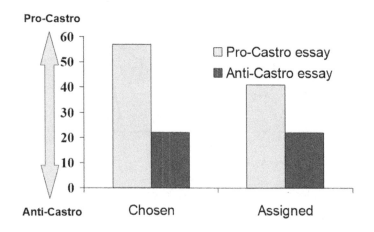

Results of Jones, Harris (1967). Logic demands that the bars in the assigned condition should have the same height.

A Matter Of Culture And Vision

Choi, Nisbett (1998) used the above approach to analyze cultural differences in the actor-observer bias. They expected that for people raised in the highly individualistic Western culture, the effect should be stronger than for those who absorbed the more collectivistic perspective of Asian cultures. The researchers presented anti- and pro-capital punishment essays to 101 students from the University of Michigan and to the same number of students from the So-Gang university in Seoul, noting that in some cases the authors were free to choose their position and in other cases were assigned a side. After reading the essays, the participants were asked to estimate the true attitude of the author towards capital punishment. The results confirmed the actor-observer bias as well as the expectations of the researchers. While both the American and Korean students identified a pro-capital punishment attitude in authors who had been asked to write a pro-capital punishment essay, and thus were not given a choice, the effect was more pronounced among American students than their Korean counterparts.

This is in line with another study (Miller 1984) that found similar cultural differences in the actor-observer bias when comparing attributions made by children about negative actions by other people. While American children focused on aspects of personality, Indian children tended to explain the same behavior in terms of situational circumstances. It should be noted though that the bias was only found in older children, for children below the age of eleven, the cultural difference did not surface.

Curiously, this difference even appears when participants are primed with a certain culture. Hong, Morris, Chiu, Benet-Martínez (2000) divided high-school students from Hong-Kong into three groups. Group one was shown pictures of American icons and wrote ten sentences about American culture. Participants in group two saw images of Chinese icons and were instructed to write ten sentences about Chinese culture. Group three, serving as the control group, viewed pictures of natural landscapes and wrote a short text about landscapes. Afterward, all participants read a story about a boy who decided to eat cake at a buffet dinner despite being overweight and told by physicians to quit eating food containing large amounts of sugar. Explaining the boy's behavior, the group primed with American culture put more emphasis on personality traits than the group that was primed with the Chinese culture.

At this point we should mention that recent publications, in particular the thorough meta-analysis of over one-hundred actor-observer asymmetry studies by Malle (2006), have shown that the bias is less robust and more limited than initially assumed. The good news: the meta-analysis confirmed the existence of the actor-observer bias for negative events (angry outburst, failing a test) as well as situations in which actor and observer were in a more intimate relationship. The effect was also likely to surface when the actor was perceived by the observers as rather idiosyncratic. However, here come the bad news, in case of positive events (helping a stranger, losing weight) the actor-observer bias proved to be much weaker than expected and on numerous occasions even appeared in a reversed fashion, meaning that now the actors use personality traits and the observers situational forces to explain behavior.

The suprising reversal of the effect in case of positive events may be the result of an interaction of the actor-observer bias with yet another human weakness experiments have brought to light: the self-serving bias. When you take the time to help an old lady cross the street, your self-esteem certainly profits more from explaining this good-natured behavior in terms of your unrivaled friendliness (personality trait) instead of just favorable circumstances (situational forces). It seems that the constant need to bolster one's self-esteem can be powerful enough to trump the actor-observer bias. Yes, we are so horribly biased that the one bias has to fight the other bias over who gets the prime time slot ...

Now that you're convinced of the existence of the actor-observer bias, the related cultural differences and are aware of its limitations, let's have a quick look at the why. Why is it, that actors and observers assess one and the same situation so differently? One obvious factor is the information asymmetry. While the actor is aware of the events leading up to a situation and the relevant mental processes, the observer can only guess. We simply don't know what happened before the man's outburst in the restaurant and we have no idea what was going on inside his head. However, we know what events and thoughts brought us to the computer store. Another important factor, though less obvious, is the perceptual asymmetry, the literally different perspective.

As early as 1935, long before the actor-observer bias was first described, Koffka noted that we ascribe causation and importance to the objects that are most dominant in our visual field. For example, imagine two light sources pointing towards the floor in a darkened room, one stationary, one moving. The gap between the two light-points on the ground slowly grows. Which of the two light sources is moving and thus responsible for the widening gap? It turns out that subjectively, it is always the one we are looking at. We determine this light source to be the culprit for the simple reason of being dominant in our visual field.

Taylor, Fiske (1975) noted that a similar perceptual effect occurs when observing people rather than objects. In their experiments, the researchers asked participants to observe a discussion between two people seated across each other. Turns out that participants who faced discussant A deemed A to be more influential, while participants facing discussant B saw B as more influential. There was no clear favorite for those who watched the scene from the side. This result shows that the assessment of a discussant depends on how dominant this person is in the visual field of the observer. It's easy to see how this can lead to the actor-observer bias. In the actor's visual field is the situation, with all its objects and people, in the observer's visual field is first and foremost the actor (especially when he's in the middle of an angry outburst). So when psychologists say that the actor-observer bias is a consequence of differing perspective, this is meant in a quite literal, geometric sense. Even without the information asymmetry, the mere fact that we cannot see ourselves should lead to an actor-observer bias.

Let's Talk Later

A few more remarks on the actor-observer bias before we conclude the chapter and move on to the next curiosity of the mind. Cialdi et al. (1973) found that the anticipation of a discussion about a certain topic leads people to take on a more moderate position on said topic prior to the discussion. For example, a person who strongly feels about gay marriage, one way or the other, and is asked to speak at a public rally on this topic, is likely to assume a more compromising position before going on stage and addressing the crowd. This is probably a result of the human tendency to present oneself in a favorable light. Moderate opinions are generally associated with rationality, open-mindedness and stability and we surely wouldn't mind being linked to these qualities.

Could the anticipation of discussion also have an effect on the actor-observer bias? Considering Cialdi's results, this seems likely. An actor, expecting to talk about his behavior with another person, might be willing to question his situational perspective and take into account the influence of his personality traits to reach a more balanced position. Similarly, the observer can find a more balanced position by going beyond the simplistic "behavior follows traits" mantra and taking a more careful look at situational factors. These shifting positions should lead to a reduction in the magnitude of the actor-observer bias and maybe even eliminate it completely. Seems plausible, but is it true? As always, it's up to an experimental study to decide.

Wells et al. (1977) put this moderation hypothesis to the test. 96 female undergraduate students, divided into groups of two, took part in the experiment. In each group one participant was assigned the role of the actor, whose job consisted of helping a confederate to finish a task, while the other participant took on the role of the observer. Half of the participants were informed that following the completion of a questionnaire, they would meet a research trainee and discuss the session. For the other half the experiment ended with the questionnaire. The result: when participants expected no discussion, the traditional actor-observer bias surfaced, but the anticipation of discussion indeed made the actor-observer bias vanish, confirming the above train of thought. Just when you thought it couldn't get more curious ...

So what can we learn from the discussion? How can we use awareness of the bias to better ourselves? A straight-forward approach is to always picture yourself in the opposite role. If you did something that would qualify as a negative event, try to put yourself in the mind of an observer and start paying attention to the personality traits that might have caused the behavior. This can provide valuable clues on where to begin the self-improvement. On the other hand, if you acted in a positive manner, don't forget to take into account the reversal of the actor-observer bias. You might be inclined to shower yourself with the most desirable personality traits there are, helpful, compassionate or even heroic, so it's wise to have a closer look at the situational factors that caused your exemplary behavior to arrive at a more realistic self-image (your self-esteem won't be pleased though – proceed with caution). Then there's being an observer, in which case you should resist the urge to explain the actor's behavior with personality traits, as this would no doubt leave you with a very crude and overly simplistic model of reality, and focus on situational aspects instead. In short: walk a mile in his shoes.

Sources And Further Reading:

The Actor and the Observer: Divergent Perceptions of the Causes of Behavior (Edward E. Jones, Richard E. Nisbett)

Objectivity in the Eye of the Beholder: Divergent Perceptions of Bias in Self Versus Others (Emily Pronin, Thomas Gilovich, Lee Ross)

Biases in Attribution (Rajiv Jhangiani, Hammond Tarry)

Illusory Causation: Why It Occurs (G. Daniel Lassiter, Andrew L. Geers, Patrick J. Munhall, Robert J. Ploutz-Snyder and David L. Breitenbecher)

Anticipated Discussion of Interpretation Eliminates Actor Observer Differences in the Attribution of Causality (Gary L. Wells, Richard E. Petty, Stephen G. Harkins, Dorothy Kagehiro and John H. Harvey)

Dunning-Kruger

I am fascinated by people's flaws and delusions: all the messy bits of human nature we all try to pretend we don't have.

– Hattie Morahan

Unskilled And Unaware

In 1999, Justin Kruger and David Dunning recruited 45 undergraduate students from Cornwell university for a study exploring logical reasoning skills (or so the unsuspecting students were told). The questions were taken from a Law School Admissions Test preparation guide. After completing the test, each participant was asked to provide information on three additional items. Firstly, the researchers wanted to know where the student placed himself relative to his peers in terms of general logical reasoning ability. The response was given in form of a percentile ranking (any number between 0 and 100 with 0 being the worst, 50 exactly average and 100 the best). Secondly, they asked the participants to estimate their relative test performance, again in percentile form. Finally, the students were asked to estimate how many of the 20 test items they got right. This is where the experiment ended for the participants and the work of the researchers began.

On the whole, the participants did well on estimating how many of the questions they got right, 13.3 perceived correct versus 12.9 actually correct, but greatly overestimated both their general reasoning ability and test performance relative to their peers. This is curious, however, the real story is provided by the breakdown of the scores. While the actual test performance of the bottom quartile (0th to 24th percentile) was on average in the 12th percentile, they believed their test performance to be in the 62nd percentile – a gross overestimation, going from considerably below average to noticeably above average. The same was true for students in the 2nd quartile (25th to 49th percentile). Their test performance relative to other participants was in the 32nd percentile, but they saw themselves in the 64th percentile. The students in the 3rd quartile (50th to 74th percentile) were pretty accurate in assessing their relative test performance, while the participants who landed in the top quartile (75th to 100th percentile) underestimated it, going from the impressive 86th percentile to the more humble 68th percentile, which is quite close to where the low performers believed themselves to be. So while actual test performance varied significantly, the perceived test performance did not. Low performers greatly overestimated and high performers underestimated their place on the percentile scale. Only the "well performers" provided realistic estimates.

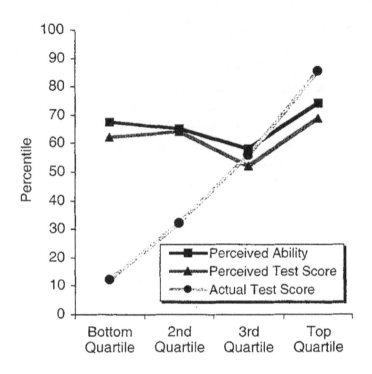

Results of Kruger, Dunning (1999)

This is an impressive demonstration of what became known as the Dunning-Kruger effect: the incompetent don't realize their level of incompetence, the competent don't realize their level of competence (for different reasons though – more on that later). Several follow-on studies confirmed this. Right after their logical reasoning experiment, Kruger and Dunning invited another 84 Cornwell university undergraduates to take part in a grammar study. Again the students completed a 20-item test, containing questions on English grammar taken from a National Teacher Examination preparation guide, and were asked to rate their performance relative to their peers. The results were pretty much the same. Participants in the bottom quartile scored in the 10th percentile, but saw themselves in the 61st percentile. At the other end of the spectrum there were the high performers who fell in the 89th percentile, but considered themselves to be in the 70th percentile. Only the well performers in the 3rd quartile got it right again and provided a realistic estimate of their performance.

Before we go on, a quick remark on the rather unpleasant word "incompetent", which is frequently used when discussing the Dunning-Kruger effect. When authors talk about an incompetent participant, they mean that this participant performed poorly with respect to the narrow task given by the experiment. But we should always keep in mind that no person is incompetent in general, we all have our strengths and weaknesses. A participant who happens to perform poorly on a logical reasoning test might be great at repairing cars, playing the violin or showing compassion for other people. And a high performer on a grammar test might be utterly incompetent when it comes to solving equations or managing people. This is why I prefer the terms "low performers", "high performers" and the somewhat awkward combination "well performers" in the discussion.

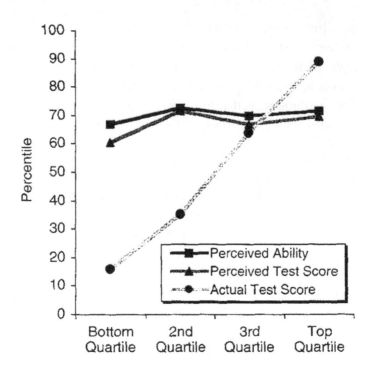

Results of Kruger, Dunning (1999)

Why the significant difference between the perception and reality? Let's focus on low performers first. Suppose you had to take a vocabulary test in French class without knowing any French words. It's clear that not only would you fail this test, you also wouldn't be able to evaluate your own test or the tests of your peers as the skills required to complete the test are also vital when trying to tell a low from a high performer. Low performance thus goes hand in hand with the inability to evaluate yourself and others and accordingly, this makes placing yourself accurately on a percentile scale impossible.

Of course, in the above hypothetical scenario you probably wouldn't overestimate your performance as the situation is pretty clear. No words means no performance. In reality things are often less clear though. Everybody can reason logically and everybody knows at least the basics of grammar. But how well one can reason and how sound one's grammar skills are is pretty difficult to say without expert feedback (which we rarely get). But the basic idea remains: if you lack the skills to reason well, you will not be able to distinguish between those who reason well and those who don't as this would require you to be able to reason well. Hence, you cannot place yourself in a meaningful manner on the percentile scale, you cannot tell if you are below- or above-average. Low performers believe themselves to be high performers because they lack the skills to identify high performers. And without the skills to realize that they are low performers, they will not see the need to improve, thus remaining low performers – a tricky situation.

Learn To Be Better

Another follow-on study by Kruger and Dunning provided compelling support for this train of thought. In this experiment 140 Cornwell students were asked to take a test containing ten logical reasoning problems based on the Watson selection task. Again, each student provided three additional data points: an estimate of his general logical reasoning skills compared to his peers (percentile), an estimate of his relative test performance (percentile) and the number of problems the student thought to have solved correctly. The analysis of the tests and additional data confirmed the expectations: low performers did not recognize their deficits, well performers provided an accurate assessment of their performance and high performers were too humble. The resulting graph is so similar to the previous graphs that I won't even bother showing them here. However, the experiment did not end here. In a next step, half of the participants, randomly selected, received a short training lesson on logical reasoning. The remaining half was given an irrelevant filler task of the same duration. After the training lesson / filler task was completed, each participant was given the opportunity to review his test and update his skill and performance assessment. Without further ado, here are the results of the untrained half:

Rating	Untrained			
	Bottom ($n = 18$)	Second ($n = 15$)	Third ($n = 22$)	Top ($n = 15$)
	Self-ratings of percentile test performance			
Before	55.2	57.9	57.5	83.1
After	54.3	58.8	59.8	84.3
Difference	−0.8	0.9	2.3	1.3
Actual	11.9	32.2	62.9	90.0
	Self-ratings of raw test performance			
Before	5.8	5.4	6.9	9.3
After	6.3	6.1	7.5	9.6
Difference	0.6*	0.7	0.6*	0.3
Actual	0.2	2.7	6.7	10.0

Their assessment hardly changed. For example, consider the bottom quartile. Before the filler task, they placed themselves in the 55th percentile, after the filler task in the 54th percentile (their actual performance fell in the 12th percentile). As for the number of correctly solved problems, the participants in the bottom percentile thought they had solved 5.8 problems before the filler task and 6.3 after completing the task (actually they had only solved 0.2). A mysterious gain in confidence, but not worth delving into. Much more interesting are the results of the participants who received the training lesson:

Trained			
Bottom (n = 19)	Second (n = 20)	Third (n = 18)	Top (n = 13)
Self-ratings of percentile test performance			
50.5	53.4	61.9	74.8
31.9	46.8	69.7	86.8
−18.6***	−6.6*	7.8	12.1*
14.5	41.0	69.1	90.0
Self-ratings of raw test performance			
5.3	5.4	7.0	8.5
1.0	4.1	8.2	9.9
−4.3***	−1.4**	1.2**	1.5*
0.4	3.3	7.9	10.0

In this case the assessment of performance changed considerably. Have another look at the low performers. Before the training lesson they saw themselves in the 51st percentile, after the training this grossly optimistic estimate vanished and the participants identified with the 32nd percentile, still quite optimistic, but certainly much closer to the actual performance that fell in the 15th percentile. This "calibration to reality" was even more pronounced for the number of problems solved. While they assumed to have solved 5.3 problems correctly before the training, the bottom quartile changed this estimate to 1.0 correctly solved problems when the training was completed, an astonishing self-correction and again a lot closer to the actual value of 0.4. We can conclude that the gain in competence via the training session did what it was supposed to do: enable the low performer to recognize the incompetence of his former self. But it was not just the low performers who profited. Every quartile of participants corrected their assessment in the right direction. The well performers became even more accurate in their assessment and the high performers realized their superiority. Note that this training session lasted only ten measly minutes, proving that even a small amount of feedback and training can make an enormous difference.

Let's turn our attention to the high performers. Why is it that they underestimate their relative performance or, in other words, overestimate the level of competence of their peers? Are they just too humble? Data from the above study as well as other studies on the Dunning-Kruger effect shows that while the high performers underestimate their level of knowledge relative to their peers, they are quite accurate at estimating absolute performance, that is, the number of correctly answered questions. If their miscalibration was indeed just a result of being too humble, we should expect them to underestimate both. So given the data, a more likely explanation is provided by a psychological phenomenon we have already discussed: the false consensus effect. The high performers project their ability to correctly solve the problems onto their peers, leading them to believe that such a high level of competence is quite common and that their place on the percentile scale is lower than it actually is.

While the research into the Dunning-Kruger effect is still relatively young and plenty of open questions remain, it has been replicated numerous times in many different settings and thus seems to be a rather robust phenomenon. Here are a few examples to convince you of its commonness and universality. Pazicni and Bauer (2013) identified the effect across nine General Chemistry classes, collecting a total of 3668 perceived / actual exam score pairs in the process. Edwards, Kellner, Sistrom and Magyari (2003) demonstrated that clerks evaluating their performance were no more accurate than the participants in Kruger and Dunning's experiments. Haun, Zeringue, Leach and Foley (2000) showed the existence of the effect for medical lab technicians evaluating their on-the-job expertise. And even more worrisome, Pavel, Robertson and Harrison (2012) found the effect among sixty-seven aviation students from the Southern Illinois University taking a pilot knowledge test. Better not think about that next time you are sitting in a plane ...

Now that we know what the Dunning-Kruger effect is, we should also have a quick look at what it is not. A commonly found claim is that the phenomenon can be accurately summarized by the phrase "the less competent, the more confident", a tempting and catchy formula that might even agree with your real-life experiences. However, this is not at all what Kruger and Dunning discovered. To see this, have another look at the experimental results. Despite their overly optimistic self-assessment, the least competent actually turned out to be the least confident in the grammar study (though not by much). And in case of the logical reasoning study, the low performers were also less confident than the high performers. The Dunning-Kruger effect makes no claim whatsoever on who is the least and who is the most confident. All it states is that low performers tend to be too confident in assessing their abilities and the high performers not confident enough. Who comes out on top in terms of confidence is another story.

Statistical Artifacts And Task Difficulty

We should note that there is reason to believe that a portion of the Dunning-Kruger effect, though most certainly not all of it (see Ehrlinger at al. 2009), is statistical consequence rather than the mind's doing. In simple terms: the low performers overestimate their performance partly because there is much more room to overestimate than to underestimate. A similar argument applies to the high performers. We'll demonstrate this idea using a simplistic thought experiment. Assume that all people, independent of competence, have the same difficulty in assessing their relative performance, say plus / minus 30 percentiles. Now suppose that during an experiment, the low performers ended up in the 13th percentile, roughly the center of the first quartile. With a plus / minus 30 percentile error in assessing relative performance, they will believe themselves to be between the 0th and 43rd percentile, the rounded average of which is 22. So while their actual performance fell in the 13th percentile, the mere fact that there is not enough room to underestimate would bring the perceived performance to the 22nd percentile – statistically induced overconfidence.

Let's apply the same argument to the high performers. Again we assume their actual performance to be in the center of the fourth quartile, which is 88. Given the plus / minus 30 percentile error in assessing relative performance, they would place themselves between the 58th and 100th percentile, with an average of 79. Hence, while the actual performance lies in the 88th percentile, the "error ceiling" provided by the top percentile (you just can't be better than the best) would lead the perceived performance to be closer to the 79th percentile. With our assumption of a plus / minus 30 percentile error, the averages of the 2nd and 3rd quartile performers would not be affected. Below you can see the graph resulting from our crude thought experiment. It visualizes a statistical component of the Dunning-Kruger effect, that is, a component which arises from uncertainty in assessment even in absence of any psychological biases. The larger the error interval, the more pronounced this miscalibration would be. It should be noted that the statistical portion of the Dunning-Kruger effect does not end with the uncertainty in assessment. Researchers also have to take into account a rather sneaky statistical phenomenon called regression to the mean. However, to keep the text flowing and to avoid getting lost in technicalities, we will banish the discussion of this phenomenon to the appendix.

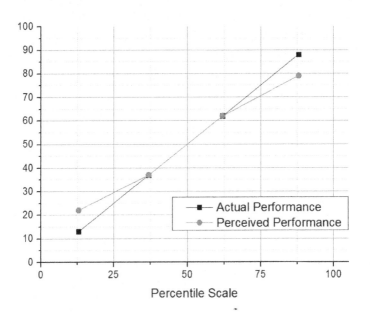

Statistical component of the Dunning-Kruger effect

Another important aspect of the Dunning-Kruger effect is its dependency on task difficulty (Burson et al. 2006). In the studies we have discussed in detail here, the well performers have always been right on target. However, this is not always the case as the amount of miscalibration can shift considerably with task difficulty. When a task is perceived as particularly simple, everyone is inclined to put himself in the top spot. Hence, participants across the board treat themselves to some extra percentiles, making the self-assessment of low performers (and possibly the well performers as well) less accurate and that of the high performers more accurate. On the other hand, in case of tasks that are seen as rather difficult, participants are inclined to go easy on the percentiles, driving the low performers closer to their actual performance score and the high performers away from it. The graph below illustrates this dependency on task difficulty. Note that all the data is purely hypothetical and only serves to visualize the shift.

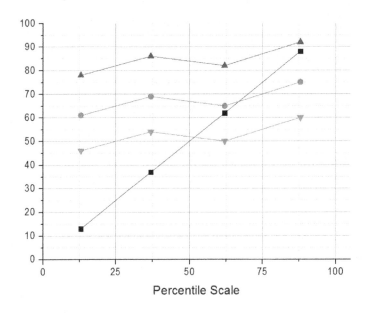

Perceived performance with varying task difficulty (pink = high task difficulty, red = moderate task difficulty, blue = low task difficulty)

Before concluding the chapter, we should mention that there is an intimate connection between the Dunning-Kruger effect and another, more general, psychological effect referred to as the above-average bias or illusion of superiority. The above-average bias states that people tend to overestimate their own qualities and abilities relative to others. There are many fascinating examples of this. For instance, Svenson (1981) found that 93 % of American drivers consider their driving abilities to be better than average. Swedish drivers turned out to be a bit more humble with 66 % saying that the average driver is no match for them. Another classic study (Cross 1977) showed that not even the academic elite is immune to the above-average delusion. A whopping 94 % of college professors said that their teaching skills are above average. Even more absurd: a significant majority of people believes that they are less susceptible to biases than the average person (Pronin, Lin, & Ross, 2002). Oh, the irony ... The connection to the Dunning-Kruger effect is pretty straight-forward. Usually a larger number of participants will overestimate their performance rather than underestimate it, leading to the unfortunate result that the majority of participants see themselves as performing above average. Only in case of particularly high task difficulty will the above-average effect vanish or even reverse.

Sources And Further Reading:

Unskilled and Unaware of It: How Difficulties in Recognizing One's Own Incompetence Lead to Inflated Self-Assessments (Justin Kruger and David Dunning)

Why the Unskilled Are Unaware: Further Explorations of (Absent) Self-Insight Among the Incompetent (Joyce Ehrlinger, Kerri Johnson, Matthew Banner, David Dunning and Justin Kruger)

Characterizing illusions of competence in introductory chemistry students (Samuel Pazicni and Christopher F. Bauer)

The Dunning-Kruger Effect and SIUC University's Aviation Students (Samuel R. Pavel, Michael F. Robertson and Bryan T. Harrison)

The Hobgoblin of Consistency: Algorithmic Judgment Strategies Underlie Inflated Self-Assessments of Performance (Elanor F. Williams, David Dunning and Justin Kruger)

Flawed Self-Assessment: Implications for Health, Education, and the Workplace (David Dunning, Chip Heath and Jerry M. Suls)

Placebo Effect

There is a major problem with reliance on placebos, like most vitamins and antioxidants. Everyone gets upset about Big Science, Big Pharma, but they love Big Placebo.

– Michael Specter

A Little White Lie

In 1972, Blackwell invited fifty-seven pharmacology students to an hour-long lecture that, unbeknownst to the students, had only one real purpose: bore them. Before the tedious lecture began, the participants were offered a pink or a blue pill and told that the one is a stimulant and the other a sedative (though it was not revealed which color corresponded to which effect – the students had to take their chances). When measuring the alertness of the students later on, the researchers found that 1) the pink pills helped students to stay concentrated and 2) two pills worked better than one. The weird thing about these results: both the pink and blue pills were plain ol' sugar pills containing no active ingredient whatsoever. From a purely pharmacological point of view, neither pill should have a stimulating or sedative effect. The students were deceived ... and yet, those who took the pink pill did a much better job in staying concentrated than those who took the blue pill, outperformed only by those brave individuals who took two of the pink miracle pills. Both the effects of color and number have been reproduced. For example, Luchelli (1972) found that patients with sleeping problems fell asleep faster after taking a blue capsule than after taking an orange one. And red placebos have proven to be more effective pain killers than white, blue or green placebos (Huskisson 1974). As for number, a comprehensive meta-analysis of placebo-controlled trials by Moerman (2002) confirmed that four sugar pills are more beneficial than two. With this we are ready to enter another curious realm of the mind: the placebo effect, where zero is something and two times zero is two times something.

The Oxford Dictionary defines the placebo effect as a beneficial effect produced by a placebo drug or treatment, which cannot be attributed to the properties of the placebo itself and must therefore be due to the patient's belief in that treatment. In short: mind over matter. The word placebo originates from the Bible (Psalm 116:9, Vulgate version by Jerome) and translates to "I shall please", which seems to be quite fitting. Until the dawn of modern science, almost all of medicine was, knowingly or unknowingly, based on this effect. Healing spells, astrological rituals, bloodletting ... We now know that any improvement in health resulting from such crude treatments can only arise from the fact that the patient's mind has been sufficiently pleased. Medicine has no doubt come a long way and all of us profit greatly from this. We don't have to worry about dubious healers drilling holes into our brains to "relieve pressure" (an extremely painful and usually highly ineffective treatment called trepanning), we don't have to endure the unimaginable pain of a surgeon cutting us open and we live forty years longer than our ancestors. Science has made it possible. However, even in today's technology-driven world one shouldn't underestimate the healing powers of the mind.

Before taking a closer look at relevant studies and proposed explanations, we should point out that studying the placebo effect can be a rather tricky affair. It's not as simple as giving a sugar pill to an ill person and celebrating the resulting improvement in health. All conditions have a certain natural history. Your common cold will build up over several days, peak over the following days and then slowly disappear. Hence, handing a patient a placebo pill (or any other drug for that matter) when the symptoms are at their peak and observing the resulting improvement does not allow you to conclude anything meaningful. In this set-up, separating the effects of the placebo from the natural history of the illness is impossible. To do it right, researchers need one placebo group and one natural history (no-treatment) group. The placebo response is the difference that arises between the two groups. Ignoring natural history is a popular way of "proving" the effectiveness of sham healing rituals and supposed miracle pills. You can literally make any treatment look like a gift from God by knowing the natural history and waiting for the right moment to start the treatment. One can already picture the pamphlet: "93 % of patients were free of symptoms after just three days, so don't miss out on this revolutionary treatment". Sounds great, but what they conveniently forget to mention is that the same would have been true had the patients received no treatment.

There are also ethical consideration that need to be taken into account. Suppose you wanted to test how your placebo treatment compares to a drug that is known to be beneficial to a patient's health. The scientific approach demands setting up one placebo group and one group that receives the well-known drug. How well your placebo treatment performs will be determined by comparing the groups after a predetermined time has passed. However, having one placebo group means that you are depriving people of a treatment that is proven to improve their condition. It goes without saying that this is highly problematic from an ethical point of view. Letting the patient suffer for the quest of knowledge? This approach might be justified if there is sufficient cause to believe that the alternative treatment in question is superior, but this is rarely the case for placebo treatments. While beneficial, their effect is usually much weaker than that of established drugs.

Another source of criticism is the deception of the patient during a placebo treatment. Doctors prefer to be open and honest when discussing a patient's conditions and the methods of treatment. But a placebo therapy requires them to tell patients that the prescribed pill contains an active ingredient and has proven to be highly effective when in reality it's nothing but sugar wrapped in a thick layer of good-will. Considering the benefits, we can certainly call it a white lie, but telling it still makes many professionals feel uncomfortable. However, they might be in luck. Several studies have suggested that, surprisingly, the placebo effect still works when the patient is fully aware that he receives placebo pills.

Experimental Evidence

One example of this is the study by Kaptchuk et al. (2010). The Harvard scientists randomly assigned 80 patients suffering from irritable bowel syndrome (IBS) to either a placebo group or no-treatment group. The patients in the placebo group received a placebo pill along with the following explanation: "Placebo pills are made of an inert substance, like sugar pills, and have been shown in clinical studies to produce significant improvement in IBS symptoms through mind-body self-healing processes". As can be seen from the graph below, the pills did their magic. The improvement in the placebo group was roughly 30 % higher than in the no-treatment group and the low p-value (see appendix for an explanation of the p-value) shows that it is extremely unlikely that this result came to be by chance. Unfortunately, there seems to be a downside to the honesty. Hashish (1988) analyzed the effects of real and sham ultrasound treatment on patients whose impacted lower third molars had been surgically removed and concluded that the effectiveness in producing a placebo response is diminished if the patient comes to understand that the therapy is a placebo treatment rather than the "real" one. So while the placebo-effect does arise even without the element of deception, a fact that is quite astonishing on its own, deception does strengthen the response to the placebo treatment.

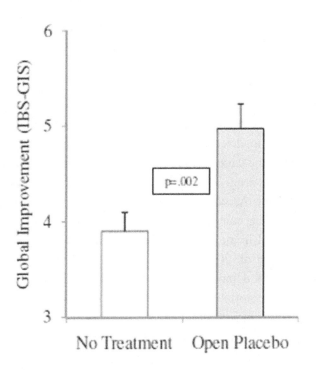

Results of Kaptchuk et al. (2010)

Let's explore some more experimental studies to fully understand the depth and variety of the placebo effect. A large proportion of the relevant research has focused on the effect's analgesic nature, that is, its ability to reduce pain without impairing consciousness. Amanzio et al. (2001) examined patients who had undergone thoracotomy, a major surgical procedure to gain access to vital organs in the chest and one that is often associated with severe post-operative pain. As handing out sugar pills would have been irresponsible and unethical in this case, the researchers found a more humane method of unearthing the placebo effect: the open-hidden paradigm. All patients received powerful painkillers such as Morphine, Buprenorphine, Tramadol, ...

However, while one group received the drug in an open manner, administered by a caring clinician in full view of the patient, another group was given the drug in a hidden manner, by means of a computer-programmed drug infusion pump with no clinician present and no indication that the drug was being administered. This set-up enabled the researchers to determine how much of the pain reduction was due to the caring nature of the clinician and the ritual of injecting the drug. The results: the human touch matters and matters a lot. As can be seen from the graph below, every painkiller became significantly more effective when administered in an open fashion. Several follow-on studies (Benedetti et al. 2003, Colloca et al. 2004) confirmed this finding. This demonstrates that the placebo effect goes far beyond the notorious sugar pill, it can also be induced by the caring words of a professional or a dramatic treatment ritual.

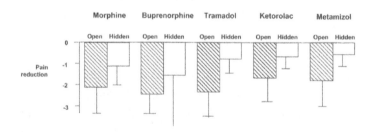

Results of Amanzio et al. (2001)

The fact that the human touch is of major importance in any clinical treatment, placebo or otherwise, seems pretty obvious (though its power in reducing pain might have surprised you). Much less obvious are the roles of administration form and treatment ritual, something we shall further explore. For both we can use the following rule of thumb: the more dramatic the intervention, the stronger the placebo response. For example, several studies have shown that an injection with salt-water is more effective in generating the placebo effect than a sugar pill. This is of course despite the fact that both salt-water and sugar pills do not have any direct medical benefits. The key difference lies in the inconveniences associated with the form of delivery: while swallowing a pill takes only a moment and is a rather uncomplicated process, the injection, preparation included, might take up to several minutes and can be quite painful. There's no doubt that the latter intervention will leave a much stronger impression. Another study (Kaptchuk et al. 2006) came to the exciting conclusion that a nonsensical therapeutic intervention modeled on acupuncture did a significantly better job in reducing arm pain than the sugar pill. While the average pain score in the sham acupuncture group dropped by 0.33 over the course of one week, the corresponding drop in the sugar pill group was only 0.15. Again the more dramatic treatment came out on top.

The experimental results mentioned above might explain why popular ritualistic treatments found in alternative medicine remain so widespread even when there are numerous studies providing ample proof that the interventions lack biological plausibility and produce no direct medical benefits. Despite their scientific shortcomings, such treatments do work. However, this feat is extremely unlikely to be accomplished by strengthening a person's aura, enhancing life force or harnessing quantum energy, as the brochure might claim. They work mainly (even solely) because of their efficiency in inducing the mind's own placebo effect. Kaptchuk's study impressively demonstrates that you can take any arbitrary ritual, back it up with any arbitrary theory to give the procedure pseudo-plausibility and let the placebo effect take over from there. Such a treatment might not be able to compete with cutting-edge drugs, but the benefits will be there. Though one has to wonder about the ethics of providing a patient with a certain treatment when demonstrably a more effective one is available, especially in case of serious diseases.

Don't Forget Your Lucky Charm

This seems to be a great moment to get in the following entertaining gem. In 2010, Damish et al. invited twenty-eight people to the University of Cologne to take part in a short but sweet experiment that had them play ten balls on a putting green. Half of the participants were given a regular golf ball and managed to get 4.7 putts out of 10 on average. The other half was told they would be playing a "lucky ball" and, sure enough, this increased performance by an astonishing 36 % to 6.4 putts out of 10. I think we can agree that the researchers hadn't really gotten hold of some magical performance-enhancing "lucky ball" and that the participants most likely didn't even believe the story of the blessed ball. Yet, the increase was there and the result statistically significant despite the small sample size. So what happened? As you might have expected, this is just another example of the placebo effect (in this particular case also called the lucky charm effect) in action.

OK, so the ball was not really lucky, but it seems that simply floating the far-fetched idea of a lucky ball was enough to put participants into a different mindset, causing them to approach the task at hand in a different manner. One can assume that the story made them less worried about failing and more focused on the game, in which case the marked increase is no surprise at all. Hence, bringing a lucky charm to an exam might not be so superstitious after all. Though we should mention that a lucky charm can only do its magic if the task to be completed requires some skill. If the outcome is completely random, there simply is nothing to gain from being put into a different mindset. So while a lucky charm might be able to help a golfer, student, chess player or even a race car driver, it is completely useless for dice games, betting or winning the lottery.

Let's look at a few more studies that show just how curious and complex the placebo effect is before moving on to explanations. Shiv et al. (2008) from the Stanford Business School analyzed the economic side of self-healing. They applied electric shocks to 82 participants and then offered them to buy a painkiller (guess that's also a way to fund your research). The option: get the cheap painkiller for $ 0.10 per pill or the expensive one for $ 2.50 per pill. What the participants weren't told was that there was no difference between the pills except for the price. Despite that, the price did have an effect on pain reduction. While 61 % of the subjects taking the cheap painkiller reported a significant pain reduction, an impressive 85 % reported the same after treating themselves to the expensive version. The researchers suspect that this is a result of quality expectations. We associate high price with good quality and in case of painkillers good quality equals effective pain reduction. So buying the expensive brand name drug might not be such a bad idea even when there is a chemically identical and lower priced generic drug available. In another study, Shiv et al. also found the same effect for energy drinks. The more expensive energy drink, with price being the only difference, made people report higher alertness and noticeably enhanced their ability to solve word puzzles.

Figure. Pain Ratings by Voltage Intensity

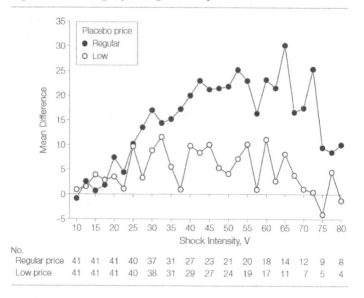

Results of Shiv et al. (2008). The graph shows the difference in pain rating before and after taking the placebo pill. Pain reduction was much stronger for expensive pills.

There is so much more to discover, we could just go on and on with the curious experimental results. For example, Branthwaite and Cooper's extensive 1981 study, based on more than 800 female participants, found that even packaging plays a vital role in drug effectiveness, both for placebos and active drugs. Pills handed out in flashy, brand-name packages turned out to be significantly more beneficial than those in bland, neutral boxes, even if there was absolutely no pharmacological difference between the pills. By the way, this effect was shown to go beyond medicine. You can make wine taste better if you give it a fancy French name and put a sophisticated-looking label on the bottle. No wonder companies invest so much money on marketing and design …

Another interesting placebo response is the nocebo effect, the name given to adverse reactions to placebo pills and treatments. Side-effects of placebos can range from feeling uncomfortable to dizziness, vomiting and even insomnia. A 2014 meta-analysis by Mitsikostas showed that around 1 in 20 patients who had received placebos during clinical trials on depression dropped out because of such adverse reactions. In 2006 a patient enrolled in such a clinical trial tried to overdose on the depression medications. After taking almost thirty pills, he began to feel faint and his blood pressure dropped rapidly. Doctors had to stabilize the suicidal man by administering intravenous fluids. Luckily, the man was part of the placebo group and had only received inert sugar pills. The nocebo symptoms vanished once the man learned that the pills were placebos and contained no active ingredient. Of course such adverse reactions can't be attributed to the properties of the placebo and must thus be a result of a person's beliefs.

Poor Little Albert

But enough with the curious results. Let's move on to the why. What causes the placebo and nocebo effect to appear? And: is it only in the mind or are there physiological components to it? We'll begin with the first question. Major psychological factors in generating the placebo effect seem to be expectancy and classical conditioning. In several placebo studies the expectations of participants have been recorded using questionnaires before the placebo treatment was initiated and the results compared to the patient's placebo response. One of the first studies that took this approach of measuring and manipulating expected pain levels (Montgomery, Kirsch 1997) concluded that expectancy accounted for roughly 50 % of the variance in pain ratings. Furthermore, statistical analysis of the collected data revealed that conscious expectation of pain reduction is necessary for the analgesic placebo effect to occur. Follow-on studies (Price et al. 1999) have confirmed this conclusion, though they found that expectancy accounted for only around 30 % of the variance in pain ratings.

Another psychological factor capable of giving rise to the placebo effect is classical conditioning. It is, in short, the linking of two stimuli using association to produce a learned response. An often-cited, though no doubt highly unethical example of classical conditioning is the so-called Little Albert experiment conducted by Watson and Rayner (1920). At the tender age of nine months, little Albert was brought into a room and shown a white rat. The boy did not respond to the rat in a particular manner, he neither displayed fear nor keen interest. But he did burst into tears as a reaction to what happened seconds later: a man struck a steel bar with a hammer not far behind little Albert's head. Over the following eleven months the procedure was repeated several times. Albert was brought in, the white rat presented, the steel bar struck with the hammer. And every time poor Albert left the room crying. Needless to say, whenever Albert came across a white rat after the eleven month conditioning period, he showed signs of fear even if no one hit the steel bar. A phobia was created, the researchers had successfully linked the sight of the white rat to the experience of fear. There's no certainty of what became of little Albert after the experiments, but one can assume that he never grew rather fond of white rats. We should note that today such an experiment would be considered unethical by the American Psychological Association's ethic code and would not be allowed to take place. For a less sinister example of classical conditioning, have a look at Pavlov's famous dogs. However, we shall return to the placebo effect now.

Most of the studies that demonstrate the power of classical conditioning in inducing the placebo effect have focused on nonhuman animals. For example, Herrnstein (1962) repeatedly injected rats with amphetamine to establish an association of the process of injection with the effects of the drug in the animals. As one might suspect, when the rats were given an injection of salt water after the conditioning period, the placebo injection did indeed result in behavior similar to that produced by the amphetamine. But making the placebo effect appear in this manner also works in humans as Goebel et al. (2002) showed. In this study, eighteen male volunteers were given doses of cyclosporin A, an immunosuppressant drug, together with 150 milliliters of aromatized strawberry milk every twelve hours for four consecutive days. During this time the participants learned to associate the immune-suppressing effects of the drug with the taste of the milk. On the fifth day the game changed: without telling the volunteers, the sneaky researchers got rid of the drug, but kept the regular doses of milk. These placebo doses then produced immune-suppressing effects comparable to those of the actual drug.

There is one final question to consider before concluding the chapter: is it all in the mind or does the placebo effect have measurable, physical manifestations? Let's think about what such a physical manifestation might look like in the case of placebo analgesia. Medical research has shown that whenever we experience pain, our body initiates the production of endorphins, an opiate substance that interacts with compatible receptors in our brain to reduce the perception of pain. This is why opiate drugs such as morphine or heroin work so well as painkillers (though, unfortunately, these substances are highly addictive and come with dangerous side-effects). Could it be that the placebo effect is related to the production of these endorphins? Do our expectations somehow manage to activate the body's opiate production facility? In 1978, long before the time of sophisticated real-time brain scans that could answer this question in a straight-forward manner, Levine et al. came up with a clever way of testing this compelling hypothesis. In their experiment the researchers found that Naxalone, an opioid antagonist, was able to considerably weaken or even completely suppress pain reduction via placebos. Several follow-on studies confirmed this result. This was a first and strong indication that the placebo effect is not just in the mind. Absolute certainty came with modern medical technology. Using positron emission tomography, Zubieta et al. (2005) were able to directly observe the placebo-induced release of endorphins, a clear physical manifestation.

The fact that not all instances of placebo analgesia could be suppressed using the opioid antagonist Naxalone led scientists to theorize that the placebo effect generally consists of an opioid and a non-opioid component. Which component takes on the dominating role depends mainly on which psychological factor, expectancy or classical conditioning, led to its formation (Amanzio, Benedetti 1999). When the placebo effect arises as a result of expectations, the opiate component dominates and the effect can thus be weakened or even eliminated using Naxalone or any other opioid antagonist. However, when the placebo response is a result of classical conditioning, the effect possesses a non-opioid character and is insensitive to Naxalone and the likes.

I'll leave you with one final note on the placebo effect. Many people, among them not just laymen but plenty of medical professionals as well, believe that the placebo effect is an indication of hypochondria. They argue that any person who gets better after receiving an inert sugar pill or sham treatment clearly did not have any medical condition in the first place. This idea is most certainly not correct. In this chapter we have encountered several experiments that successfully induced the placebo effects in participants suffering from a real medical condition (irritable bowel syndrome) or participants undeniably experiencing real pain (thoracotomy, electric shocks). Also, this perspective does not take into account the reach of the placebo effect beyond the medical field (alertness, lucky charm effect).

Sources And Further Reading:

A Comprehensive Review of the Placebo Effect: Recent Advances and Current Thought (Donald D. Price, Damien G. Finniss, and Fabrizio Benedetti)

The Placebo Effect (Spanda Journal II, 1/2001)

Placebos without Deception: A Randomized Controlled Trial in Irritable Bowel Syndrome (Ted J. Kaptchuk, Elizabeth Friedlander, John M. Kelley, M. Norma Sanchez, Efi Kokkotou, Joyce P. Singer, Magda Kowalczykowski, Franklin G. Miller, Irving Kirsch and Anthony J. Lembo)

Placebos and Painkillers: is Mind as Real as Matter? (Luana Colloca and Fabrizio Benedetti)

Commercial Features of Placebo and Therapeutic Efficacy (Rebecca L. Waber, Baba Shiv, Ziv Carmon, et al.)

Behavioral Conditioning of Immunosuppression is Possible in Humans (Marion U. Goebel, Almuth E. Trebst, Jan Steiner, Yu F. Xie, Michael S. Exton, Stilla Frede, Ali E. Canbay, Martin C. Michel, Uwe Heemann and Manfred Schedlowski)

Chameleon Effect

I have a lot of chameleon qualities, I get very absorbed in my surroundings.

– River Phoenix

Just A Harmless Fly

Encounters with wasps or bees can be a pretty painful experience for would-be predators. Their ability to sting is feared by many species in the animal kingdom. These species have learned that whenever you see the characteristic yellow and black patterns, you better run (or fly). There is one species that is particularly happy about this collective association: the harmless and rather defenseless hover fly. Why, you ask? Because it has developed the same characteristic color pattern and even imitates the wasp's stinging action when in danger. In the course of a lengthy trial-and-error evolutionary process, the hover fly has come to the conclusion that you don't need the gun as long as you look and act like you are armed to the teeth. This is mimicry at its best. And it works.

Dangerous bee or harmless fly? Better not find out! (It's a hover fly)

For humans, pretending to be someone else is much simpler. A criminal can put on an expensive-looking suit and try to pass himself off as a legitimate businessman by learning a few clever-sounding buzzwords (my favorites being "synergy", "streamlining", "proactive" and "paradigm shift"). This might not fool everyone, after all, body language is a vital part of communication and quite difficult to change, but it might just fool people long enough to get away with the cash and start a new persona. But this sort of mimicry on a conscious level is not what we are interested in here. We want to explore the sub-conscious version of the phenomenon, also referred to as the chameleon effect, a classic example being the contagious effect of smiling. You have probably noticed this many times. When someone smiles, people automatically smile back (Bush, Barr, McHugo, Lanzetta 1989). Take a look at photos or, better yet, videos showing smiling faces and try to suppress the automatic reaction. You will notice that this is next to impossible. Your face muscles feel compelled to form the smile and you really have to focus hard to avoid it from happening. But then again, why would you want to suppress it, you should never pass up an opportunity to smile. By the way: this automatic reaction is the reason why we have to endure the annoying canned laughter, an informal term for prerecorded laugh tracks, frequently found in TV shows. Several experiments, among them Fuller, Sheehy-Skeffington (1974), have shown that canned laughter makes the audience laugh longer, more often and rate the material as funnier.

Smiling and laughing is only a small part of the picture though. Many studies (for example McIntosh 2006) have shown that we generally reproduce facial expressions when interacting with another person. This automatic facial matching commonly goes unnoticed by both the speaker and the listener and happens very rapidly, within one second or less, which is why scientists refer to them as rapid facial reactions (in short RFRs). Rapid facial reactions have been linked to many important social qualities such as helping and generosity (McIntosh et al. 1994). They also play a vital role in the ability of recognizing another person's emotional state (Neidenthal, Brauer, Halbertstadt, Innes-Ker 2001), a fact that might be explained by self-perception theory. As noted in the section on the IKEA effect, we commonly believe that behavior follows traits, but many experiments have indicated that this is by no means a one-way street. It seems that we also continuously observe our own behavior and deduce from that our qualities and emotional state. Hence, matching a person's facial expression can be of great help when trying to reproduce a person's emotional state.

The proposed social-emotional importance of RFRs is underlined by another interesting experimental result. McIntosh, Reichmann-Decker, Winkielman and Wilbarger (2006) found that individuals suffering from autism, a disorder associated with noticeable difficulties in social interaction as well as deficits in verbal and non-verbal communication, lack such automatic facial responses. Abashev-Konstantinovsky (1937) revealed that the same is true for people who have been diagnosed with schizophrenia. This absence of RFRs has been proposed as a core problem in autism and might explain why it is so difficult for autistic (and schizophrenic) individuals to behave in a socially acceptable manner.

One question remains: are these RFRs mere motor responses, a direct perception-action link bypassing any emotional systems, or rather a result of a person's quickly adapting emotional state? According to a thorough experiment conducted by Moody et al. (2007), there seems to be an emotional component to the phenomenon. The researchers found that when participants were put into a heightened state of fear, they showed a greater facial response to faces with fearful or angry expressions. These intensified RFRs were not observed when the fear-primed participants were shown faces with expressions unrelated to fear. This result, confirmed by Moody et al. in a follow-on experiment, indicates that RFRs are not simply exact motor reactions to facial stimuli but strongly influenced by a person's emotional state. In short, we're not just emotionally-hollow parrots (well, that's a relief). Though it's true that everyone automatically smiles back, you are more likely to reproduce a smile in full if you are happy to begin with. It seems that again we're back to the feedback loop: smiling makes us happy and being happy makes us smile more. But just as smiling is just a small part of facial mimicry, facial mimicry is just a small part of the chameleon effect as a whole. So let's find out what else we mimic subconsciously.

Now 10 % More Likable

At the top of the list, there is speech. There are numerous experimental studies establishing a definite connection between the many different aspects of speech and subconscious mimicry. Using automated recordings, Webb (1972) showed that interviewees adjust to their interviewers' speech rate. Talk faster and your dialogue partner will do the same. Just a few years later, Giles and Powelsand (1975) found that the same is true for accents. This conclusion agrees well with my personal experience of living in a region where the proper High German meets its Swiss German offshoot as well as my native dialect, the closely related Allemanisch (useless side-note: this dialect is still spoken by a few Amish groups in the US). You tend to switch automatically to the other person's accent, sometimes to achieve a certain effect, other times without even noticing it. Analyzing twelve 20-minute dyadic conversations, Cappella and Planalp (1981) extended this astonishing link between speech and mimicry by demonstrating that people also imitate each other's speech rhythms as well as the duration of pauses. And if all of this isn't enough to convince you, consider this experimental result: Buder (1991) found that we even mimic another person's fundamental vocal frequency. So the tendency to mimic speech goes a lot deeper than one might expect.

Also very high on the list is mannerism and posture. It is amazing how much we do subconsciously while sitting and talking (or just waiting): crossing our legs, inspecting our fingernails, picking real or imaginary lint off our clothing, stroking our chin, scratching / nodding / tilting our head, tapping our foot, the list goes on and on. Even when sitting, we are on the move all the time. And we can do all of this in many different postures: alert, relaxed, aggressive, defensive, dominant, submissive, exhausted, … Numerous studies, among them Bernieri (1988), have shown that people commonly mimic mannerism and posture. When you tap your foot (careful, this might annoy some people), there's a good chance your dialogue partner will sub-consciously do the same. And if you assume a defensive position, the other person will probably go on the defensive as well.

Even more amazing than the many forms of mimicry is the fact that mimicry seems to be closely connected to (mutual) liking and familiarity. One of the first studies that delved into this interesting line of research was Lafrance (1979). He discovered that not only do students mimic their instructor's postures, but that the level of sympathy the students feel for their instructor depends on the degree of posture sharing. The more they mimic their instructor, the more they like him. Or is it that the more they like him, the more they mimic? Whatever the case, Maurer and Tindall (1983) backed up the fundamental link between mimicry and positive evaluation by showing that counselors who mimic their clients are perceived as more empathetic by said clients. The often-cited Chartrand and Bargh (1999) study confirmed the link once more.

For the experiment, the researchers invited seventy-eight male and female participants and asked them to complete a 15-minute task with the help of a confederate. The confederate was instructed to either mimic the participant or display neutral mannerisms. As you might have guessed, the participants were not informed of this arrangement and believed the task, which consisted of describing various photographs, to be the central aspect of the experiment. After completing the task, all participants were asked to report how much they liked the confederate (on a scale from 1 = extremely dislikable to 9 = extremely likable) and how smoothly the interaction had gone (1 = extremely awkward to 9 = extremely smooth). The results: the average rating for liking turned out to be 6.62 in the mimicry condition and 5.91 in the control condition, a 12 % difference. As for the smoothness of the conversation, the researchers found the average rating 6.67 in the mimicry condition and 6.02 in the control condition, an 11 % difference. Both results were shown to be statistically significant or, in other words, very unlikely to be caused by random fluctuations. So it seems that mimicking another person makes you roughly ten percent more likable – that's good to know!

A few more remarks on this remarkable experiment. Outside judges, who later watched the video recordings of these interactions, did not consider the mimicker to be more likable than the non-mimicker. This indicates that only the person who is mimicked assigns the mimicker a higher likability. I guess that makes sense … The researchers were also on the lookout for gender differences, however, none were found. So we can assume that both men and women are affected by the chameleon effect to a similar degree. And here's another noteworthy result of the experiment: only one of the thirty-seven participants in the mimicry condition noticed that the confederate displayed similar mannerisms. But even this one participant did not identify the similarity in behavior as deliberate mimicry or come to realize what the experiment was really about (in which case his data would have been excluded from the analysis - for good reasons).

It's All About Empathy

In the same study, Chartrand and Bargh describe another experiment that was aimed at determining individual differences in subconscious mimicry. Since many of the earlier studies on the chameleon effect had pointed towards a deep connection between empathy and mimicry, the researchers theorized that people with a highly empathetic personality generally show a greater tendency to mimic their dialogue partners than people with little empathy for others. To test this hypothesis, Chartrand and Bargh invited another fifty-five participants and presented them with a personality test (the Interpersonal Reactivity Index developed by Davis) to measure their ability to take the perspective of other people, a quality that is vital to empathetic behavior. Then they repeated the experiment described above with minor changes and compared the tendency to mimic with the outcomes of the personality test. The results strongly support the hypothesis that as empathy grows, so does subconscious mimicry.

Chartrand and Bargh's study demonstrates that mimicry can lead to a more positive evaluation, but does this work the other way as well? Does a greater mutual liking and familiarity result in more subconscious mimicry? This seems probable, but as always in the world of science, every hypothesis, no matter how plausible, has to be put to the test.

For this we turn to Jefferis, van Baaren and Chartrand (2003). In their experiment, every participant was asked to enter into a conversation with a confederate. The participant and confederate took turns asking and answering a series of scripted questions. In roughly half of these conversations the scripted questions remained strictly impersonal, while in the other half the questions grew more personal over time, creating a sense of familiarity. The confederate was instructed to shake her foot throughout the conversation and the response of the participants to this mimicry stimulus was recorded. The subsequent analysis showed that as the questions became more personal, the level of subconscious mimicry significantly increased, confirming our expectations: more familiarity leads to more mimicry.

We should mention that the social aspect of the chameleon effect goes far beyond the individual level. Yabar, Johnston, Miles and Peace (2006) invited thirty-two female undergraduate students, all of whom identified as non-Christian, and showed them videos of confederates describing various photographs. To keep the participants busy and prevent them from thinking about the true nature of the experiment, they were led to believe that they had to describe the photographs featured in the videos to other participants after completing the task. The confederates were instructed to touch their own faces while talking about the photographs. While some confederates were given a neutral appearance, the other confederates wore items that clearly identified them as Christians (a large crucifix around the neck, a fluorescent wrist bracelet with the words "Got God" on it). As you might have guessed, the researchers were not really interested in the photographs. Their plan was to record and analyze the level of mimicry displayed by the students while watching the videos. The data showed that the (non-Christian) participants were more likely to mimic the neutral confederate than the Christian-looking confederate. This experiment, as well as several other studies that arrived at a similar conclusion (Wegner, Crano 1975 / Goodman, Gareis 1993), extend the aforementioned link between familiarity and mimicry beyond the individual level: we are more inclined to mimic people that we perceive to be members of our own group.

Now that we are convinced of the existence of subconscious mimicry and its connection to social qualities such as liking and familiarity, let's see how the effect can be put to good use in real-world situations. We have already seen that mimicry can be helpful for counselors trying to establish a relationship with their clients. And in their study titled "Mimicry for money: Behavioral consequences of imitation", Van Baaren et al. (2003) found that waiters and waitresses can use mimicry to increase the size of their tips by over 60 %. Another study by Van Baaren et al. (2004) demonstrated that the chameleon effect can induce more helpful behavior in general.

Guéguen (2007) focused on a particularly interesting application: dating. The French researcher organized speed-dating sessions that included female confederates. Some of the women were asked to mimic their dates, while the others displayed neutral behavior. By now you probably know where this is going: men who met with a confederate who mirrored their speech and mannerisms considered the interaction to be more positive and expressed greater desire to meet the woman again. Another noteworthy result of this study: the nature of the mimicry (only verbal, only non-verbal, both) did not make a significant difference. For our final example we stick to Guéguen (2007). In the experiment, four sellers were told to either mimic or not mimic the customers who showed interest in their products. When leaving the store, the customers who had interacted with one of the four sellers were approached and asked to evaluate the experience. As you might have guessed, the mimicking sellers left a considerably better impression on the buyers. On top of that, buyers who were mimicked were more inclined to go along with the seller's suggestions. So I guess the conclusion here is that no matter what the situation and no matter what the task: mimic. Or better yet: try to become even more empathetic towards your fellow men and women by taking the other person's perspective whenever possible, listening carefully to what is being said and offering help whenever needed. This will organically turn you into a better mimicker.

Let's take a moment to think about the why. Why is it that we mimic others and why does mimicry affect our judgment? In their study, Lakin, Jefferis, Cheng and Chartrand (2003) proposed that mimicry played an important role in the evolution of man. Our chances of survival clearly profit from being part of a group of people and this was especially true when humans were still living in the wild. Our ancestors had to count on their peers to help fight off dangerous animals, build shelter, collect food and reproduce. This required communication even before the development of language. But how to communicate if speech is not an option? How to express the desire to be part of a group if you can't make use of words? Here only non-verbal communication, which includes mimicry, can do the trick. As we have seen, sympathy and familiarity can be expressed by mimicking the other person's mannerisms and postures.

So it seems plausible that mirroring the scratching of the beard or shaking of the foot was our ancestor's preferred way of saying "I am part of your group". Granted, it's a stretch, but at the same time a very compelling argument. And if the theory is indeed correct, it should be no surprise that for the modern day human, mimicry is automatic and subconscious. Evolution has fixed this behavior in our brains to ensure the survival of man.

Sources And Further Reading:

Mimicry in Social Interaction: Its Effect on Human Judgment and Behavior (Nicolas Guéguen, Celine Jacob and Angelique Martin)

The Chameleon Effect: The Perception-Bahvior Link and Social Interaction (Tanya L. Chartrand, John A. Bargh)

More Than Mere Mimicry? The Influence of Emotion on Rapid Facial Reactions to Faces (Eric J. Moody, Daniel N. McIntosh, Laura J. Mann and Kimberly R. Weisser)

Moving to the Speed of Sound: Context Modulation of the Effect of Acoustic Properties of Speech (Hadas Shintel, Howard C. Nusbaum)

The Chameleon Effect As Social Glue: Evidence For The Evolutionary Significance Of Nonconscious Mimicry (Jessica L. Lakin, Valerie E. Jefferis, Clara Michelle Cheng and Tanya L. Chartrand)

The Impact Of Social Context On Mimicry (Patrick Bourgeois, Ursula Hess)

Music and the Mozart Effect

I think music in itself is healing. It's an explosive expression of humanity. It's something we are all touched by. No matter what culture we're from, everyone loves music.

– Billy Joel

Tones and Overtones

Music is all around us. We wake up to our cell phone's music clip or whatever song the radio station happens to be playing at the time our alarm clock goes off. We get into the car and automatically turn on the radio. In restaurants and shops there is a constant stream of soothing background music. When working out in the gym, energetic techno beats help us in maintaining the one-hundred watt power output until the desired amount of undesired calories is burned (hopefully never to be seen again). Finally getting home, we put in the Harry Potter DVD and subconsciously listen to the grand orchestral symphony in the background while enjoying the shenanigans of Harry, Ron and Hermione. After that it's time to finish writing that report to the upbeat and stimulating music of Mozart. Taking a bath, we put on atmospheric yoga music to help us reach a state of deep relaxation, only to be interrupted by the fantastic drum beats in the distance signaling the start of Carnival time. And when the clock strikes midnight on the thirty-first of December, we sing "Should old acquaintance be forgot ..." to greet the new year. Do I need to go on?

Have you ever stopped to wonder what music is? Have you tried to define it? Thought about why it is so omnipresent? Tried to understand what it is that makes the phenomenon music so attractive across time and culture? I have and it seems that the more you think about it, the more puzzling the phenomenon music becomes. Let's start with the purely physical picture and expand from there. When you pluck a guitar or violin string, the string begins to oscillate rapidly. This rapid back-and-forth motion is transmitted to a resonator (the hollow wooden body of the instrument) that turns the relatively weak sound into a more powerful one. As the resonator moves in one direction, it compresses the air in front of it, creating a region of higher air density which then propagates outwards. When the direction of the resonator's motion reverses, a low density region is formed that follows the propagation of the high density disturbance. The process then begins to repeat as the direction of motion is reversed once more. So the oscillation of the resonator produces a series of high and low density disturbances in the air that travel towards your ear at a constant speed of around 1200 kilometers per hour (or 760 miles per hour). This is the sound wave. Note that it's not the air that is moving towards you, but rather the density fluctuations in it. Your ears pick up these rapid variations in air density and send this information to your brain. Once the brain is finished doing its magic, you are able to "hear" the changes in density produced by the string as a well-defined tone. This seems like a pretty odd way of perceiving variations in a physical quantity, don't you think? But it gets even stranger.

Suppose that instead of just one string, you pluck two strings at the same time. Again the motion of the string will lead to the formation of density disturbances in the air that travel towards your ear. However, this time the changes in density picked up by your ears are much more complex since they are a result of the superposition of two sound waves. Your brain, being the amazing machine it is, can deal with that though. Just like the spectrum analyzers found in modern music software, it is able to identify the two distinct tones making up this complex pattern. On top of that, your brain will also let you know whether you should perceive the given combination of sound waves as pleasing or as discordant. For some reason that does not seem to lie purely in the physical realm, we perceive a combination of density fluctuations having the frequencies 523 Hz (note C) and 659 Hz (note E) as harmonic and a combination of the frequencies 523 Hz (note C) and 554 Hz (note C#) as dissonant. The one frequency mix somehow "feels right", the other doesn't, a rather curious fact.

Of course, this is not news. Pythagoras, born in 570 BC, and his followers already noted that not all musical intervals have the same psychological effect. The intervals most pleasing to the human ear are the octave, the fifth (for example, note C and G) and the third (note C and E). There are a few other intervals that are perceived as somewhat pleasing, but feel "incomplete": the second (note C and D), the fourth (note C and F) and the sixth (note C and A). The remaining intervals are rather dissonant. Many explanations have been proposed for this natural preference for certain combinations of frequencies, but no single theory can fully explain the phenomenon. The key to unlocking the secret might lie in the overtones. To understand what overtones are, we need to take a closer look at how a string produces sound.

Say we pluck a string and it produces the note C that lies at 523 Hz. This means that the string completes 523 oscillations during one second. After a short while, a node (a stationary point) appears on the string and instead of going back and forth as a whole, one half of the string now moves in one direction, while the other half moves in the opposite direction (see image below). This is a natural process in the dynamics of the string's motion. The node thus "cuts" the oscillation in half and this accelerates the frequency to $2 \cdot 523$ Hz = 1046 Hz – a new tone appears (the note C one octave higher, to be specific). But it doesn't end there as after another short while a second node appears, cutting the oscillation into three parts and producing another tone at $3 \cdot 523$ Hz = 1569 Hz (note G). In a similar fashion, more and more different tones are produced by the same string, however, at a much lower volume than the original note (which is why we usually don't perceive the extra notes consciously).

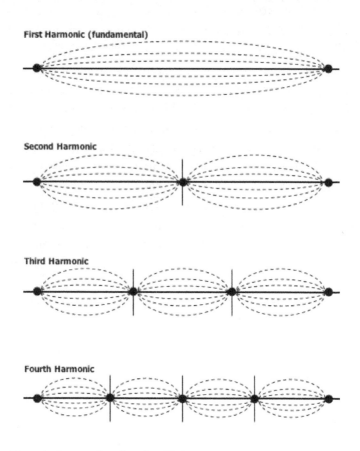

The string's natural modes of oscillation

Here's the interesting part. We know, and have known long before understanding the dynamics of the string, that the octave, fifth and third are the musical intervals perceived as most pleasing. Physics has revealed that these particular intervals also happen to be the first intervals appearing in the overtone series. Coincidence? This is pretty unlikely. Every time a string is plucked, the octave, fifth and third naturally appear and even though we might not notice the presence of the additional notes in a conscious manner, it seems much more likely that these intervals feel so pleasing because we are so used to the frequency combinations. This explanation is in line with another psychological effect called the mere exposure effect that states that people tend to like something more after being exposed to it several times ("familiarity breeds liking").

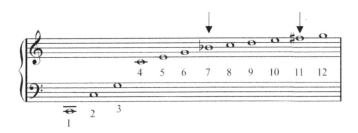

Overtone series to C. Note that with the first overtone (2) the octave appears, with the second overtone (3) the fifth and with the fourth overtone (5) the third. The arrows indicate approximations.

Music And Your Mind

But enough with the overtones, let's go back to the big picture. We now know what a tone is from a physical point of view and found a plausible explanation for why we like some combination of tones more than others. But we still haven't discussed the most basic question: what is music? This is the point where you usually insert the universally accepted definition of a term. However, there is none. Ask ten musicians and music theory experts and you'll get twenty different definitions. I think most of us would agree that the sound coming from a car engine is not music while a symphonic composition by Mozart most certainly is. But where to draw the line? Where does noise end and music start? In 1952 the American experimental composer John

Cage wrote a piece called 4'33" which consists of four minutes and thirty-three seconds of silence and nothing else. Is this music? What about a composition that consists of just a single tone being played for one minute? Music? What if instead of one tone we had three being played in a repeating pattern? And what about drum solos, should we call them music? As you can see, trying to find the line is pretty difficult. So let's give up the idea of finding a proper, all-encompassing definition and rather note the elements commonly found in what the majority of people would refer to as music: rhythm, melody, texture (for example, chords in the background played by strings or a guitar) and pattern. Different genres focus on different elements. While Hip-Hop has a strong emphasis on rhythm, classical music and ballads are usually all about melody and texture. And pieces meant to remain in the background or provide an atmospheric touch are characterized by the absence of rhythm and melody.

[By the way: I think it's an absolutely fascinating feat of the mind that we are able to talk about something without even knowing what it really is. We say that the sound coming from a car engine is not music and Mozart's piece is, and we say this with almost absolute certainty, yet when asked what music is, it seems impossible to find a satisfying answer. Isn't that absurd? The same is true for so many other concepts. We can't define consciousness, but somehow we still manage to philosophize about it all day long. Just another curiosity of the mind.]

There might not be a satisfying answer to what music is, but what we can analyze and even measure is the effect of music on the listener. For this we have a look at the experimental study "Effects of Musical Tempo and Mode on Arousal, Mood, and Spatial Abilities" by Husain et al. (2002). The researchers were interested in finding out how music affects arousal, which refers to the degree of physiological activation ranging from tired to excited, and mood, which are long-lasting emotions ranging from depressed (negative) to happy (positive). To this end, Husain et al. recorded and prepared a classical piece, the first movement of Mozart's sonata K. 448, in four versions that differed in tempo and musical key: fast-major, slow-major, fast-minor, slow-minor. The fast version had a tempo of 165 beats per minute, the slow version 60 beats per minute. In their paper the researchers note that these particular tempos were chosen because they were the fastest and slowest tempos that still sounded natural. Thirty-six students, most of them women, from the York University served as the participants.

Distinction between arousal and mood (Hu 2010)

Each participant was assigned one version of the piece and was given the The Profile of Mood States (POMS) test before and after listening to the music to assess their arousal and mood. The students also had to complete a spatial reasoning task before being debriefed. The subsequent statistical analysis of the data showed two things: 1) tempo affects arousal, but seems to have no effect on mood and 2) musical key affects mood, but has only a small effect on arousal. So the tempo of a song determines whether you become more tired or more excited whereas the key makes you either more depressed or happier. No doubt this influence on arousal and mood is one of the reasons why music is so attractive and omnipresent. It can cheer us up when we're down in the dumps, it can calm us down when we are nervous. Of course you probably suspected that before reading this text. But it's always nice to see something we consider to be plausible or maybe even obvious confirmed by hard data.

We should note that the results of Husain et al. (2002) are in line with numerous other experimental studies which set out to analyze the effects of music on emotion, some of which even measured the physiological responses to music in addition to administering self-reporting tests. Krumhansl (1997) for example found that listening to music induces changes in heart rate, skin temperature, respiration and hormone secretion that are similar to those shown to other emotional stimuli. And Brown et al. (2004) showed that the exposure to music activates the same regions of the brain that light up when a person experiences intense emotions: the thalamus, hippocampus, amygdala, prefrontal cortex, orbitofrontal cortex, midbrain/periaqueductal gray and others. So even without relying on self-reporting, a procedure which is naturally a lot more error prone and contestable than the measurement of physical quantities, the link is pretty obvious.

Say No to Marketers

We noted that the participants in the above experiment also had to complete a spatial reasoning task. This was because the researchers were not just interested in emotional effects, they also wanted to know whether music can enhance a person's cognitive abilities. The idea that music can make you smarter became very popular in the mid-nineties under the name "Mozart effect" and has remained popular ever since. The hype began with the publication of Rauscher et al. (1993) in the journal Nature. The researchers discovered that participants who were exposed to the aforementioned Mozart sonata performed better on the Stanford-Binet IQ test than those who listened to verbal relaxation instructions or sat in silence.

This revelation caused armies of mothers and fathers to storm the CD stores and bombard their children with Mozart music. One US governor ordered the distribution of Mozart CD's by hospitals to all mothers following the birth of a child. Not surprisingly, marketers eagerly joined the fun (with increasingly ridiculous claims about the effect of music on intelligence) to profit from the newly-found "get-smart-quick" scheme. What got lost in the hype however was the fact that Rauscher et al. never found or claimed that exposure to Mozart would increase your IQ in general. Neither did they claim that the performance on an IQ test is a reliable indicator of how smart a person is. All they demonstrated was that exposure to an enjoyable musical piece led to a temporary (< 15 minutes) increase in spatial reasoning ability, not more, not less. Despite that, the study suffered the fate all studies are bound to suffer when they fall into the hands of the tabloid media, politicians and marketers: the results get distorted and blown out of proportion.

By the way: I wonder if mothers and fathers would have been just as eager to expose their children to Mozart had they known about some of the less flattering pieces written by the brilliant composer, among them the canon in B-flat major titled "Leck mich im Arsch" (which translates to "Kiss my Ass") and the scatological canon "Bona Nox!" which includes the rather unsophisticated line "shit in your bed and make it burst". These are just two examples of the many obscene and sometimes even pornographic pieces the party animal Mozart wrote for boozy nights with his friends. One can picture the young composer and his companions sitting in a flat in Vienna singing obscene songs after downing a few bottles of wine while concerned mothers cover their children's ears, cursing the young generation and their vile music. That's the side of Mozart you won't get to hear in orchestral concerts.

But back to the topic. So whatever happened to the Mozart effect? Hype aside, is there anything to it? The thorough 1999 meta-analysis of Mozart effect studies by Chabris came to the conclusion that the popularized version of the effect is most certainly incorrect. Listening to Mozart, while no doubt a very enjoyable and stimulating experience, does not permanently raise your IQ or make you more intelligent. However, said meta analysis, as well as the 2002 Husain et al. study described above, did find a small cognitive enhancement resulting from exposure to Mozart's sonata.

The explanation of the enhancement turned out to be somewhat sobering though.

In the original study, Rauscher et al. proposed that Mozart's music is able to prime spatial abilities in a direct manner because of similarities in neural activation. Further discussion and experiments showed that such a direct link is rather unlikely though, especially in light of the results of Nantais and Schellenberg (1999). In this study participants performed a spatial reasoning task after either listening to Mozart's sonata or hearing a narrated story. When the reasoning task was completed, the participants were asked which of the two, Mozart's piece or the story, they preferred. The result: participants who preferred the sonata performed better on the spatial reasoning task after listening to the piece and participants who preferred the story performed better on the test after hearing the story. However, participants who listened to Mozart's music and stated that they would have preferred the story instead did not show the cognitive improvement. Overall the researchers found no benefit in the Mozart condition. All of the above implies that the enhancement in performance is a result of exposure to a preferred stimulus rather than a direct link between Mozart and cognition. It seems that the Mozart effect is just a small part of a broader psychological phenomenon that goes a little something like this: experiencing a preferred stimulus, be it a musical piece, a narrated story or a funny comic book, has a positive effect on arousal and mood and this in turn enhances cognitive abilities.

Aside from spatial reasoning, what are the cognitive abilities that can be improved by exposure to music via the preferred stimulus mechanism described above? Several experiments pointed out noticeable gains in information processing. For example, Wood et al. (1990) observed that participants finished a symbol-coding task more quickly when music was played in the background. And Kenealy (1988) noted that listening to music reduces the time needed to produce word associations as well as the time taken to come to a decision. So I guess this means that listening to "Should I Stay Or Should I Go" by the punk rock band The Clash actually helps you in deciding whether you should stay or go – who would've thought? Experiments have also revealed temporary enhancements in psychomotoric skills such as the time needed for counting and the pace at which a series of numbers is written down (Pignatiello et al. 1986 / Clark, Teasdale 1985). Even more interesting than the aforementioned cognitive enhancements are the changes in social thinking that come with the consumption of music and the associated changes in emotion. Music induces a stronger sexual arousal (Mitchell et al. 1998), leads one to rate others higher in terms of attraction (May, Hamilton 1980) and, most importantly, increases the willingness to help others (North et al. 2004). So picking up tiny fluctuations in air density produced by a vibrating string makes you more inclined to help your fellow men – yet another "who would've thought?" moment and a great place to leave you wondering what else there is to the puzzling phenomenon that is music.

Sources And Further Reading:

Effects of Musical Tempo and Mode on Arousal, Mood, and Spatial Abilities (Gabriela Husain, William Forde Thompson and E. Glenn Schellenberg)

Music and Mood: Where Theory and Reality Meet (Xiao Hu)

The Mozart Effect: Evidence For The Arousal Hypothesis (Edward A. Roth, Kenneth H. Smith)

Making Sense Of The Mozart Effect: Correcting The Problems Created By Null Hypothesis Significance Testing (Ryan M. Sweeny)

Emotional responses to music: The need to consider underlying mechanisms (Patrik N. Juslin, Daniel Vaestfjaell)

Appendix

Mean and Standard Deviation

To understand scientific papers and experimentally determined results, one needs to have an understanding of the basic parameters involved. In this section we will have a look at two fundamental quantities: mean and standard deviation. Another important quantity, the p-value, will be covered separately in the next section. The mean or average is a pretty intuitive concept and also quite easy to calculate. Suppose you've made a number of measurements (for example height of people or test results of students) and want to know the center value. This is what the mean can tell you. Denoting the individual measurements by m_1, m_2, m_3, and so on, we can compute the (arithmetic) mean m by adding all these values and dividing that sum by the total number of measurements n:

$$m = (m_1 + m_2 + m_3 + ...) / n$$

For example, suppose we are given the following test scores of five students: 45, 62, 78, 33, 47. The mean score in this sample of students is simply: $m = (45 + 62 + 78 + 33 + 47) / 5 = 53$. Generally around half of the measurements will be above this average and the other half below it, though in case of a highly asymmetric distribution it is possible that the majority of values lie above or below the mean. Note that the mean does not tell us anything about how scattered the measurements are. An average test score of 53 points could be a result of all students performing close to this mean or a result of having a few low and a few high performers with a large gap in between. Clearly, for a teacher it would be important to know which of the two scenarios he or she is dealing with. The standard deviation can be of help here.

The standard deviation SD is a measure of the variability in the data set. As a rule of thumb for symmetrical distributions, we can expect 70 % of given or further measurements to lie in the range from the mean minus one standard deviation (m – SD) to the mean plus one standard deviation (m + SD). And 95 % of measurements can be expected to lie between the mean minus two standard deviations (m – 2·SD) and the mean plus two standard deviations (m + 2·SD). This is also known as the 95 % confidence interval and is often explicitly stated in publications. So keep in mind that the greater the standard deviation, the more the measurements are spread out. We will not delve into its computation here, but if you need to calculate it, there are plenty of free online calculators that will happily do the job for you.

Let's go through an example of how to apply the concept. Suppose we measure how much engine oil a certain car model requires for a distance of one thousand kilometers eight times. We get the following data (in liters): 0.21, 0.18, 0.13, 0.19, 0.18, 0.25, 0.21, 0.19. Typing this into an online calculator, we find that the mean is m = 0.193 and the (sample) standard deviation SD = 0.034. These results imply that in 70 % of all further measurements we can expect the oil consumption to be between this lower limit:

m – SD = 0.193 – 0.034 = 0.159 liters

And this upper limit:

m + SD = 0.193 + 0.034 = 0.227 liters

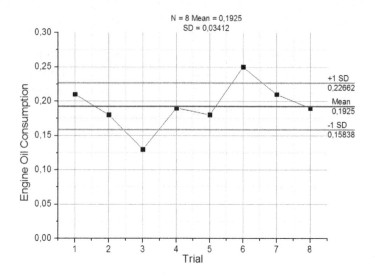

Visualization of the mean and the ± 1 standard deviation interval

The 95 % confidence interval ranges from:

$m - 2 \cdot SD = 0.193 - 0.068 = 0.125$ liters

To this upper limit:

$m + 2 \cdot SD = 0.193 + 0.068 = 0.261$ liters

The fuel consumption will rarely move outside this interval. As you can see, the standard deviation is indeed a very helpful tool in evaluating measurements. You can find a more detailed treatment, including instructions on how to calculate the standard deviation and the basics of another very important statistical quantity called the standard error of the mean, in the final chapter of my book "Statistical Snacks". However, basic knowledge in algebra and a keen interest in probability calculations are necessary for enjoying the book.

P-Values

When reading a scientific paper, you will commonly across the so-called p-values. For example, when reporting the results of their grammar study, Kruger and Dunning noted that participants overestimated the number of problems they answered correctly, with 15.2 perceived correct versus 13.3 actually correct. Without comment or explanation, this is followed by this important piece of information: $p < 0.0001$. What does it mean? In short, p-values determine the statistical significance in hypothesis tests and can thus be seen as a measure of how "strong" the result is.

In almost every scientific experiment researchers take two samples of the population, group 1 and group 2, do something and then compare the groups with respect to some parameter. They expect to see some difference between the groups due to a certain proposed effect (for example the benefits of a new drug or a new learning method). However, there are two fundamental problems the researchers have to deal with. First of all, there is the sampling bias. If you take a random sample of thirty people and measure their heights, the average height in this sample might be different from the true average height in the population for the simple reason of statistical variation. If you are lucky, your sample will be rather representative, but this will not always be the case. Not taking into account such random variations would enable you to "prove" the most adventures theories. Suppose that for some odd reason a group of researchers believes that people are shorter during the day. They take a sample of 30 random people in the afternoon and another sample of the same size at night. Now if the average height in the "day-group" turned out to be lower than that in the "night-group", could we conclude that their hypothesis is correct? Clearly we couldn't as this difference might just be a result of random variation.

The other obvious issue is the effect itself. Even if the theoretical arguments are very compelling, there's always the chance that the proposed effect is insignificant or even non-existent (the new drug is not really beneficial, the new learning method is nonsense), in which case any difference that arises is solely due to statistical fluctuation. This lack in meaningful difference is called the null hypothesis. It is basically the position a skeptical person would assume and seriously considering its truthfulness is part of any scientific study. An important tool that helps to guide researchers to the right conclusion, statistical variation or real effect, is the p-value. It expresses the probability of obtaining the given experimental difference in at least this magnitude if the null hypothesis were true, or in other words, the probability of arriving at the given difference by pure chance rather than via some real effect. The smaller the p-value is, the more confident researchers can be in ruling out random variation as an explanation. Any result with $p < 0.05$ is called statistically significant.

Let's look at one hypothetical example to absorb this concept. Suppose you believe that speed reading has a negative effect on text comprehension and you want to test this hypothesis experimentally. For this, you randomly select thirty students and train them in the art of speed reading. These students will form group 1. Another thirty randomly chosen students make up group 2. You invite them to the lab and present each participant with a handful of texts as well as corresponding text comprehension questions. Participants are then assigned a text comprehension score according to their performance. You find the following results: Average score group 1 = 73 %, average score group 2 = 88 % and $p < 0.01$. These results show that the speed readers did indeed perform worse than the non-speed readers and that there is a less than 1 % chance that the difference found by the experiment is a result of random variation rather than a real effect. This means that if the proposed effect did not exist (true null hypothesis) and you performed this experiment one thousand times, only ten or less of these experiments could be expected to find such a strong difference. So you can be relatively confident that your hypothesis is correct, but to be absolutely certain you'd have to replicate the findings.

Replication works well in reducing uncertainty because (decimal) probabilities multiply for independent events. A quick example to demonstrate the principle: if Tom shows up to the meeting with a probability of 0.5 or 50 % and John shows up with a probability of 0.2 or 20 %, then the probability of both showing up is $0.5 \cdot 0.2 = 0.1$ or 10 %. Applying this concept to experimental studies we can see that if the chance of obtaining a certain experimental result by random variation is 0.01 (1 in 100) or 1 %, then the odds of getting the same result twice by pure chance is only $0.01 \cdot 0.01 = 0.0001$ (1 in 10,000) or 0.01 %. So the replication made random variation as an explanation extremely unlikely. But if that still isn't good enough for you, a third replication will bring the chance of the result being a consequence of unfortunate sampling down to $0.01 \cdot 0.01 \cdot 0.01 = 0.000001$ (1 in 1,000,000) or 0.0001 %. This is of course assuming that the replications are independent of each other: different participants, different researchers, different labs, ... So the next time you are reading a study, be sure to pay attention to the p-value and be sure to check whether the effect has already been replicated.

Regression to the Mean

Instead of simply explaining what regression to the mean is, let me demonstrate the workings of this tricky statistical phenomenon using the following example taken from Schall and Smith (2000). The researchers looked up the ten baseball players with the highest betting averages in 1998. You can find the corresponding values in the left column of the table below. Then they looked up the betting averages of the same ten players in 1999 and compared the performance. The result: seven out of the ten players did much worse in the following year. And those three players who did manage to improve, didn't improve by much. The average decrease across the group was 33 points or roughly 10 %. What happened? Why did the performance of the top ten players deteriorate by so much? Coincidence?

1998	1999	Difference
363	379	16
354	298	−56
339	342	3
337	281	−56
336	249	−87
331	298	−33
328	297	−31
328	303	−25
327	257	−70
327	332	5

Before we try to find out what happened here and why this result shouldn't surprise us, let's take a moment to take a look at a hypothetical examination scenario. Suppose we present students with a test consisting of two sections. In section one the students have to answer ten general knowledge questions. For each correct answer a student is given one point. In section two the students have to pick a number between one and six and roll a dice. If the dice shows the number they picked, they receive one point. This game of guessing is repeated ten times. Given this set-up, the lowest possible test score is zero points (no correct answers, no correct guesses) and the highest possible score twenty points (ten correct answers, ten correct guesses). Clearly the performance depends partly on skill and partly on luck. Any student who receives a particularly high score must have been both skilled and lucky.

Now suppose a student receives eighteen points (nine correct answers and nine correct guesses) and is retested the next day. What is your prediction? Will the student's score improve, stay the same or decrease? We can assume that the performance on the skill portion won't change by much. However, it is unlikely that the student remains so lucky. So overall we can expect his score to go down. The same is true if we pick the ten students with the best performance (implying both skill and luck) and retest them. While we can expect the skill to remain on the initial level, most of them won't be so lucky on the second take. On average, the score in the group will decrease, in other words: they will regress to the mean.

The link to the aforementioned baseball players is obvious at this point: while reaching a 300+ batting average most certainly takes a lot of skill and hard work, we can assume that there is also some luck involved. The top ten players in 1998 were both highly skilled and lucky, but it's very unlikely that all of them remain so lucky in the following year. Hence, the 10 % decrease across the group should not come as a surprise. Whenever performance on a certain task depends both on skill and luck, we can expect this regression to the mean phenomenon to occur. Remember the Sports Illustrated cover jinx? It's an urban legend that states that any player or team appearing on said cover will be subject to a string of bad luck. Regression to the mean explains this "curse". Only those who perform particularly well, the highly skilled and lucky, will be featured on the cover. And while the skill will always be theirs, it is unlikely that their string of good luck can be maintained. On average, their performance will deteriorate.

Regression to the mean can lead us to see connections and patterns where there are none. For example, an instructor might claim that yelling at students after they showed a particularly bad performance on a test is an effective strategy. His experience shows that after such a "shock therapy", the performance of the student improves almost every time. But as you know by now, this is not necessarily a result of the instructor's intervention. Getting to the bottom percentiles usually requires both a lack of skill <u>and</u> an absence of luck. And while the former might not change over a short time span, the latter most likely will. Hence, on the next test we can expect the worst performing students to show an improvement, but this increase in performance cannot serve as proof that the "shock therapy" actually works. It is just another example of regression to the mean. So if you come up with some performance-enhancing treatment and want to demonstrate that your (expensive) treatment actually works, just pick the bottom ten students and let regression to the mean do its magic. You can literally prove anything with this approach and only people who are familiar with the regression to the mean phenomenon will be able to see through you.

Afterword

I have found the missing link between the higher ape and civilized man; it is we.

- Konrad Lorenz

Here are some more personal thoughts to round off the discussion. In the book you often encountered phrases such as "The participants responded by doing XYZ" or "This result shows that people tend to do XYZ". But who are these participants whose minds seem to be so easily manipulated? And who are these mysterious people who act in such a primitive and predictable manner? I hate to say it, but they are you and me. This is the one thing you should take away from this book. Look into the mirror and you will see the easily manipulated participant who starts mimicking the confederate just because she's asking questions with a more personal touch. So predictable! You, Mr or Ms soandso from soandso born in soandso in nineteen-soandso. This book was all about you, your family, your friends and even that one weird neighbor (you know who I mean).

But how can that be? Aren't we supposed to be rational beings who carefully look at the pros and cons and make a sensible and informed decision? We can be, but I wouldn't count on it. People (you and me) often base their decisions on crude heuristics. We go with what "feels" right without being able to properly express why it feels right or what that even means. We see patterns in random fluctuations and subconsciously base our thinking on the shaky conclusions resulting from that. We hit the computer keyboard when the PC freezes as if this angry outburst could accomplish anything. And it seems that at the end of the day we are driven first and foremost by what every social animal desires: survival, acceptance, status, in that order. Does all of this sound very rational to you? It's very human, that's for sure. Some people believe that humans are sophisticated and civilized beings with a small animal core, while I prefer to think of you and myself as a social animal with a thin coating of sophistication and civilization. A coating so thin that it can come off in a pretty transparent manner just because the PC freezes or the train arrives a few minutes late. With this, I leave you to your own thoughts.

Thank you, come again.

- Apu Nahasapeemapetilon

Copyright

Made in the USA
Las Vegas, NV
15 December 2022